SELF-ESTEEM

SELF-ESTEEM

the cross and christian confidence

JOANNA MCGRATH
& ALISTER MCGRATH

Inter-Varsity Press

INTER-VARSITY PRESS
Norton Street, Nottingham NG7 3HR
Email: ivp@ivpbooks.com
Website: www.ivpbooks.com

First published in 1992 by Crossway Books, UK, under the title *The Dilemma
of Self-Esteem*. This revised and expanded edition first published 2001.

Reprinted 2006, 2009

British Library Cataloguing in Publication Data
A catalogue record for this book is available from the British Library.

ISBN 978-0-85111-547-4

Set in Garamond
Typeset in Great Britain
Printed and bound in the UK by 4edge Limited, Essex

*Inter-Varsity Press publishes Christian books that are true to the Bible and that
communicate the gospel, develop discipleship and strengthen the church for its
mission in the world.*

*Inter-Varsity Press is closely linked with the Universities and Colleges Christian
Fellowship, a student movement connecting Christian Unions in universities and
colleges throughout Great Britain, and a member movement of the International
Fellowship of Evangelical Students.*
Website: www.uccf.org.uk

CONTENTS

Preface

This book was begun while the authors were based at Drew University, Madison, New Jersey, in 1990. We acknowledge with gratitude the assistance given by Drew University Library in obtaining important publications. The planning of the book took place during a period spent at Willowbank, Bermuda, and we acknowledge with pleasure the space this offered us to explore in more depth the issues raised by the book. We also wish to thank Mrs Ann Bruce for several helpful conversations on self-loss, and Dr Barrington White for pointing out the importance of the parable of the talents to our theme.

In preparing the second edition of this work, we have used material we developed for the purpose of teaching courses on the topic of 'Christian approaches to self-esteem' for a study day at the Oxford Christian Institute of Counselling and a summer school at Regent College, Vancouver, in 1995. We are grateful to the participants at both events for their helpful comments.

Alister McGrath
Joanna McGrath

Introduction

This is the second edition of a work which originally appeared in 1992, and which has been rewritten to take account of the many helpful comments received from those who used the original edition, and in response to constant enquiries from counsellors wanting to know when a new edition would appear. The work has been thoroughly revised, and it is our hope that it will prove useful to all those concerned with problems of self-esteem in Christian ministry.

Self-esteem poses a dilemma for the Christian. The 'self-esteem movement' has become of major importance in Christian circles, especially in the United States. Works such as Robert Schuller's *Self-Esteem: The New Reformation* have urged Christians to value and 'feel good' about themselves. There is a growing concern in both secular and Christian counselling to liberate individuals from an unjustified negative evaluation of themselves, which can be crippling in its consequences.

Most people have come across individuals in this situation. We once met a young woman at a church meeting. She explained that she felt she was 'nothing', totally worthless. The only reason God had sent his Son to die for her was his infinite mercy. There was nothing about her that could have moved him to do this. She looked downcast and sounded miserable. She is perhaps typical of many in the churches today who are utterly convinced of their personal worthlessness. And this sense of total worthlessness seems to lie at the root of many pastoral difficulties. It renders people unable to achieve the full potential of their calling as Christians. It inhibits them from accomplishing the tasks God may have in mind for them. Those who believe that they are 'nothing' or 'valueless' will feel that they can contribute nothing to the life of the church, and will go on to do just that. As a result, both these individuals and the church are impoverished.

The recent concern to liberate such people from their negative self-image is understandable. Yet the concern to promote positive self-esteem often seems to rest upon highly questionable theological foundations. Central Christian ideas such as the reality of sin and the demand for humility (note the stress on self-denial in the New Testament: Matt. 5:40; 18:4; Mark 8:34; 10:43–44; John 3:30; Rom. 3:23; 1 Cor. 10:24; Phil. 2:3) seem to have been abandoned or compromised. The price paid for positive self-esteem is often a dilution or distortion of the gospel. As a result, the 'self-esteem movement' has met with powerful criticism within Christian circles.

Influential writers such as Jay Adams and Paul C. Vitz have argued that the new concern for self-esteem is little more than an excuse for self-worship. Thus Adams has described self-esteem as a 'pagan' idea, which has no place in Christianity. Instead of talking about 'self-worth', we ought to think of ourselves as 'like criminals, and put self to death every day'.

So, many Christians find themselves facing a dilemma. They are confronted with one group of Christian writers who urge them to have a strongly positive view of themselves, and with another group who urge them to have an equally strong negative view of themselves. But which is right? And how has this confusing situation arisen?

This book aims to address questions relating to self-esteem fully and directly in a psychologically informed and theologically responsible manner. In part, the confusion results from a degree of psychological and theological shallowness; many of the ideas and methods of secular psychotherapy have been adopted uncritically in Christian counselling, often on the assumption that they are 'scientific' or 'unbiased', without a full understanding of some of their presuppositions and implications. It is vitally important to realize that all psychotherapeutic approaches are based on metaphysical belief systems and demand a degree of faith from their adherents. Psychoanalysis, behaviourism and humanism are all examples of belief systems that demand commitment and assent.

Throughout this work, we try to explain and relate the technical languages of both psychology and theology to a non-specialist audience without oversimplification or distortion. The central idea of this book is *self-esteem*. Although the term is familiar to most people, the idea is considerably more complex than is generally realized.

The present work argues that Christian confidence rests totally upon the cross of Christ, but that some of the therapeutic insights of modern psychology can be seen as valid in its light. For this reason, a central chapter of the book deals with the tensions between the gospel and most secular psychotherapies. It is shown that the latter often rest upon assumptions that the Christian cannot accept. The authors, a psychologist and a theologian, aim to bring together and integrate the insights of their disciplines with a view to resolving these tensions, rather than simply acknowledging their existence. For psychotherapy can be genuinely helpful to those suffering from negative self-esteem, if viewed and used in a responsibly Christian manner.

The three opening chapters of this book present an overview of the history of the idea of self-esteem, exploring how it has become of major importance in modern western culture. It is shown that self-esteem is a complex idea, involving a judgment concerning personal acceptability and worthiness to be loved, along with associated emotions. Positive self-esteem is linked with good mental health and well-adapted personality. Self-esteem is a way of experiencing present security, which has arisen through past experience of relationships, especially parenting.

These chapters thus deal with the concept, basis and maintenance of self-esteem. Although this material will be of particular interest to those who already have some knowledge of the behavioural sciences, we hope that we have made it accessible to those unfamiliar with the field. One of the reasons underlying our decision to write on the subject of self-esteem is that it is a concept of significance and meaning to both the mental health professional and the lay person. It is readily understood and relates meaningfully to human experience.

A second reason for choosing to focus on self-esteem is that we have actually found it to be an issue that is repeatedly addressed throughout Scripture, having both pastoral and theological significance. While Scripture does not use the specific term 'self-esteem', the general theme of human self-worth is unquestionably there in both Old and New Testaments. Self-esteem thus represents a topic that lends itself well to exploration from both psychological and theological perspectives.

Having dealt with psychological approaches to self-esteem, the fourth chapter considers contradictions, points of contact, and parallels between secular theoretical accounts of self-esteem (and therapeutic approaches based on them) and the Christian view of human nature. In particular, we raise the issues of the reality of sin in human nature, and the Christian calling to humility. These are potential areas of tension between Christian and secular worldviews.

It is then shown how these contradictions can be resolved through the cross of Christ. Chapter 5 explains how the cross is the objective basis of Christian self-esteem. A proper understanding of the way that Christ's death on the cross has dealt with sin and enabled salvation helps make sense of self-esteem in the life of the believer. Particular attention is paid to the idea of sin as 'separation from God', and to redemption as 'attachment to God'. Faith in the crucified Christ changes the status of the believer.

In chapter 6 the implications of attachment to God are explored in further detail. Our experience of our relationship with the Father is discussed with reference to the rich variety of scriptural images of God's loving parental care, and our status as his adopted children.

The authors have intended to be totally faithful to Scripture in dealing with these issues. To illustrate the positive manner in which our approach to self-esteem relates to the scriptural witness, chapter 7 takes the form of a reading of Paul's letter to the

Philippians. This letter deals with the outworking of a proper Christian self-esteem in the life of the individual believer. It is not simply individual biblical texts or episodes that relate to issues of self-esteem; at times, issues of self-evaluation dominate substantial sections of Scripture, as this writing indicates.

Finally, the implications of all this for the life of the whole church are explored in chapter 8. This final chapter aims to make connections between theory and practice by applying the approach to self-esteem developed in the course of this book to the everyday life of the Christian community. Suggestions are made for incorporating these insights into preaching and teaching, and we show how these insights relate to the sensitive areas of criticism and the need to value others within the Christian community.

Any work written by two authors, attempting to integrate two different disciplines, places demands on both its writers and its readers. This work represents a sustained attempt to bring together, in a helpful and responsible manner, the insights of psychology and theology as they relate to self-esteem. The book may appear to consist of psychological sections, written by a psychologist, and theological sections, written by a theologian. In fact, the work has been jointly written throughout, trying to ensure that the insights of both disciplines are addressed throughout the entire work. The authors believe there is a genuine synergy between theology and psychology in this specific area, and that understanding how they illuminate each other offers important insights for pastoral ministry.

1

The concept of self-esteem

This book explores the concept of self-esteem, a preoccupation of western culture since the late twentieth century, from a Christian perspective. The writers are a psychologist and a theologian, and the subject is approached using the methods of both disciplines.

Both psychology and theology have something to say about the way people and societies behave, and about the nature of emotional experience. Psychological and theological approaches can sometimes run alongside each other quite happily in parallel, each confined to its own specialist area. Sometimes they seem to provide complementary approaches, offering different perspectives on the same subject. Sometimes there is a tension between psychology and theology which may erupt into outright conflict.

This book attempts to use psychology and theology together in an integrated approach that interweaves insights from both disciplines and applies them to God's creation. While we have chosen to write on self-esteem, we might equally have chosen other subjects and other approaches: for instance, biology and theology. Nevertheless, psychology is particularly helpful in that it not only provides an intellectual account but can be applied to good effect in pastoral situations.

One of the authors first became interested in the idea of self-esteem when working with children who had suffered severe congenital facial deformity. Was it possible for such children to make it through from childhood to adulthood with the ability to feel good about themselves? Could they cope with the natural cruelty of other children who might taunt them about their appearance? Would they be able to handle the traumas of adolescence? Did plastic-surgery procedures that made them look significantly more 'normal' (but still left them obviously disfigured) make any difference to the way they felt about *themselves*? This is, after all, the decisive criterion of the success of such financially and emotionally costly interventions. In order to investigate such a question, it is necessary to be able to measure self-esteem in a reliable way. The first step towards measurement is definition.

The need for a definition of self-esteem

The fact that many different people can all use a particular phrase with ease, each intuitively knowing what he or she means by it, is no guarantee that they all mean the same thing in using it. Indeed, if there is one area in which people use terms vaguely and imprecisely, it is in the description of aspects of their own mental lives. In part, this is because of the subjective nature of mental events.

We could point to a sack of potatoes and say, 'Look! Those are potatoes! Let's weigh them!' Everyone looking on would see the same potatoes and understand what was being measured. Self-esteem is simply not like that. It is not tangible. We may, however, have a rough understanding of what someone else means by the term. In fact, that rough understanding may be good enough. For most purposes, it does not matter that individuals' ideas of self-esteem are not identical, as long as they are related. Using this term may help us to understand and express our interior experiences and to make sense of our observations about other people.

But the lack of a precise definition of self-esteem – both what it *is* and what it *does* – becomes very important indeed in other contexts. It is vital to have an agreed precise definition of the term when we set ourselves the task of developing a formal explanatory theory of the behaviour of others, or of developing techniques for changing that behaviour. Most significant of all, we must understand what is meant by self-esteem when we prescribe what constitutes psychological health. In other words, there must be agreement at least on what is defined as 'healthy' if we are to prescribe the directions in which people judged to be 'unhealthy' should change.

Several issues should be noted here. *First, a failure to define self-esteem means that theories relating to it cannot be tested rigorously against experimental evidence.* If the idea of self-esteem is left vague or undefined, experimental evidence that threatens any inadequate theory about psychological health could be accommodated by broadening or changing the emphasis of the concept. The goal-posts can be moved.

Secondly, it is possible that self-esteem (or, more accurately, negative self-esteem) is merely an elaborate name for something else, such as depression. There is indeed some evidence that low self-esteem and depressed mood have significant features in common. As a result, measures of one can 'contaminate' measures of the other, simply because they are closely related. Unless we can give a tight and precise definition of self-esteem, which carefully distinguishes it from related ideas (such as depression), we might end up doing little more than adding an extra piece of unnecessary jargon to an already complex field of study.

Thirdly, if self-esteem is defined too broadly, it could lose any real significance as a distinctive idea. In some ways, this develops the point just made in the previous paragraph. For example, high self-esteem could be understood to mean all that is good, and low self-esteem all that is bad, about human nature. Such a ubiquitous concept carries no information. In an attempt to explain every-thing, it can come to mean nothing. This seems to be a danger inherent in the approach of Robert Schuller in his work *Self-Esteem: The New Reformation* (1982). Schuller here defines self-esteem as 'the human hunger for the divine dignity that God intended to be our emotional birthright as children created in his image'.

So how can such a subjective notion of self-esteem be defined? One approach is to *operationalize* the concept. In other words, we state which observable external behaviours reflect the internal workings of the personality. To give an example, we might say that a person with negative self-esteem[1] would be expected to say things such as 'I am not good enough ...' on a fairly regular basis, so that its probability can be measured and used as a guide to self-esteem. The subjective internal notion of self-esteem is thus understood to be reflected in things that that person says or does, which can be seen and noted by an observer.

A precise behavioural description may thus be achieved, but some would argue that the essence of self-esteem has evaporated in the reduction process! While this point has to be acknowledged, it cannot be used as an excuse to evade the responsibility of devising testable theories of human behaviour. An operationalized concept may be limited in some respects, but it can nevertheless be a useful tool.

Those in the enormously responsible position of counselling people who are emotionally weak and vulnerable must ensure that the theories they use to evaluate and assist their clients are tested to the limits and are reliable and effective. We have the same responsibilities as an airline which expects its customers to trust in the safety of its aircraft. Both the airworthiness of the aeroplane and the aerodynamic theories that undergird its design are tried and tested. Psychological therapists must not evade the same obligation.

Thus, our first task is to define clearly what is meant by self-esteem in the context of the argument developed in this book. To do this, it is necessary to examine briefly the origins and development of the concept in modern psychology.

---

[1] Throughout this book, we have tended to use the terms *positive* and *negative* self-esteem, rather than *high* or *low* self-esteem. There are two reasons for this.

First, the terms 'high' or 'low' self-esteem carry with them the idea of a *unidimensional* concept (analogous to temperature or weight). As will become clear from our discussion later, self-esteem may equally be thought of as a multidimensional concept (like health) involving a variety of factors, which must be considered in terms of quality as well as quantity.

Secondly, the terms 'high' or 'low' self-esteem might be thought to imply that self-esteem is a *continuously varying* concept (again, like temperature or weight). It may be more helpful to think of self-esteem as *dichotomous* – *either* intact or impaired, in much the same way as human beings can be described simply as either 'male' or 'female' (rather than varying degrees of male or female).

William James

The nineteenth-century American psychologist William James (1843–1910) was probably the first to employ the experimental psychological, rather than the philosophical, approach to the study of the self. This essentially biological approach was influenced by the evolutionary theory of Charles Darwin (1809–82), which stresses the continuity between humans and other animal species. James pointed out the paradoxical nature of our being able to stand back from ourselves and view our own consciousness as a subject of study. (Some contemporary psychologists term this process *metacognition*.) James found it necessary to distinguish two aspects of the self: self as the *known* and the self as the *knower*. This capacity for self-consciousness is probably closely related to the development of language. As such, it is arguably unique to humankind.

James believed that each person's 'self-concept' is the view of the known self that is held by the knower. The known self has material, social and 'spiritual' (temperamental) components – such as 'being tall', 'being a footballer' or 'being easy-going' respectively. The self-concept develops as the knower watches each of these components at work, especially in interactions with other people. Indeed, other peoples' descriptions may also be incorporated into the concept of self. The self-concept is a neutral description of a person, but it is usually embedded in a value system incorporating ideals and aspirations. The value system modifies the self-concept, giving it a judgmental nature.

For example, the description of the self as 'a skilled footballer' might imply approbation in a culture that values sporting success. However, if the aspirations of the person and those around him or her are concerned with academic excellence (to the exclusion of all other achievements), then exactly the same description could be damning. Value systems affect the way we see ourselves.

One of the authors clearly recalls an incident from her school days when, after stumbling her way unsuccessfully through a reading assignment, a dyslexic girl was asked to explain her poor performance. She defended herself by telling the teacher that she was good at practical things, such as needlework and cookery. The teacher (who had been educated at Cambridge University) responded by saying that she was *disgusted* with the girl. In another context the girl's practical achievements might have been highly valued. This incident illustrates the way a value system influences the meaning placed on one's actions.

Once an evaluative judgment is made about the self which goes beyond the neutral descriptions entailed in the self-concept, feelings become involved. These feelings are pleasant if the judgment is good and unpleasant if the judgment is bad.

Thus as early as 1890, James had introduced three vitally important points about the nature of self-esteem:

1. Self-esteem depends upon the making of *value judgments* about the self.

2. Both the self-concept and the value judgments made about it are closely related to the views of other people.

3. The making of value judgments, either critical or affirming, is accompanied by an emotional response.

Freudian psychoanalysis

The Viennese psychologist Sigmund Freud (1856–1939), founder of the psychoanalytic school, formulated important theories about the development of the personality and the origins of neurosis (disordered or maladaptive behaviour). His theories of child development are based not on systematic observations of children, but rather on the retrospective accounts of his neurotic adult clients. Furthermore, Freud did not conduct formal experimental tests of his theories. Thus, although the theories are often set out in pseudo-scientific terms, they can in no sense be considered scientific. Indeed, one of the main criticisms of the psychoanalytic approach has been that it is extremely difficult, if not impossible, to test its validity or to demonstrate the efficacy of the treatment procedure.

However, there is no doubt that Freud's prolific writings have not only deeply influenced the development of western psychology; they have also had a profound effect on the way ordinary people think about the human mind. The theories are creative and were innovative, and they make a significant contribution to the topic of self-esteem.

Freud's theories are complex and can be outlined only briefly here. (For more detailed treatment, the reader is referred to the select bibliography at the end of this book.) What follows is a simplified account of his ideas relating to self-esteem. Freud viewed the human mind or *psyche* as a closed energy system directed by instincts (predominantly the sexual instinct). He held that three systems are at work in the adult personality: the *id*, *ego* and *superego*. The interaction between these is complex and changing. As a result, the personality is *dynamic*, rather than fixed or static. (Theories of this type are often referred to as *psychodynamic*.)

The *id* is an unconscious system that operates according to the pleasure principle; that is, it works towards immediate gratification or reduction of tension.

The *ego*, which begins to develop at about six months of age, is a conscious system. It tries to direct and control the id and is rational in character.

The *superego*, which develops some time after the age of four, is partly conscious. It strives towards attaining a morally acceptable model personality. It is formed by a process of identification with significant others, usually the parents.

Freud viewed early experience as vitally important in shaping the adult personality. The developing child is seen as passing through a series of stages, each of which is defined by the part of the body through which pleasure is most easily derived and the id gratified. The early stages are very much concerned with the gaining of pleasure from the self, rather than from external objects or people.

The abnormal adult personality may have become stuck or *fixated* at an early developmental stage, or it may *regress* to an early developmental stage as a result of psychological trauma. An example is the concept of *narcissism* or narcissistic personality disorder. Freud viewed the narcissistic person as stuck in an infantile world in which self-love is dominant, where the ultimate in sexual fulfilment is masturbation. This person lacks empathy towards others and may use them, but is obsessed by his or her own power, importance or brilliance. There may be a preoccupation with envy of others, but no love of others. For this sort of person, the superego has never developed or is somehow lost. Conversely,

Freud describes clients suffering from depression who have abnormally low self-regard. For such people, the ego has become empty.

As the child passes through each stage of development, he or she will experience frustration, anxiety and conflicts. The child uses ego strategies to deal with these difficulties. The strategies determine the adult personality. Where the strategies are inappropriate, neurotic or unhealthy behaviour will emerge.

One important strategy is *identification*. This is the process by which an external object or person becomes incorporated into the personality. As noted above, this strategy underlies the emergence of the superego, and occurs as a response to the male Oedipus complex. Put simply, the child desires his mother sexually, but is frightened of his father. This conflict is resolved by the identification with the father; the child vicariously possesses the mother, but avoids paternal retribution. The values and attributes of the father become part of the developing child's personality. The child can begin to say to himself and to his thoughts, 'That's naughty', rather than relying entirely upon parental correction of his actions.

Lastly, it is important to note Freud's development of the idea of *defences*. These are strategies used by the ego to protect the personality from psychological threat and to reduce anxiety. One example is repression – that is, to push an anxiety-producing object into the subconscious so that it does not have to be faced. Such strategies can preserve mental health, but they are also frequently blamed for holding back adequate personal growth. Narcissism itself has been described by some psychoanalytic writers as a defence against low self-esteem. This potentially confusing area will be described in more detail later.

Freud acknowledged that individuals evaluate themselves. One role of the superego is to be the 'self as knower'. He also emphasized the introjection or internalization of the views of others in forming this evaluative system. Freud introduces the idea that abnormalities in self-regard may underlie some mental-health problems or inadequate personality function. He also introduces the notion that certain mental strategies provide protection for the personality or maintain the *status quo*.

Post-Freudian ego psychology and cognitive psychology

The post-Freudians developed many of Freud's concepts, but they also changed the emphasis of much of his teaching. Alfred Adler (1870–1937), an early associate of Freud, eventually rejected the primacy of the sexual drive as an explanation for all behaviour. He placed more emphasis upon the goal-directedness of human behaviour and the aggressive drive to achieve. The pathological expression of such striving may be found in the *inferiority complex*. This term has found its way into everyday use, and it bears some relation to the concept of chronically low self-esteem.

One of the main thrusts of post-Freudian psychology was to give the ego the executive function denied to it by Freud and to cease to see the ego as a slave to instincts. In other words, the conscious ego is seen as much less controlled by unconscious instincts, and as able to function in a directive manner. People are viewed as more actively in control of their own lives. This psychology moved away from examining distant childhood or subconscious origins of neurosis towards considering how ego-controlled adult behaviours maintain neurosis here and now.

The importance of valuing the self and taking responsibility for action is stressed. The aim of psychotherapists such as Karen Horney (1885–1952) is therefore to change the way a client views the self in order to improve the quality of interaction with others. 'Being unable to accept himself as he is, [the client] cannot possibly believe that others, knowing him with all his shortcomings, can accept him in a friendly or appreciative spirit.'

One development of this 'ego psychological' approach is found in the work of the cognitive behaviour therapists such as Albert Bandura (1925–), Albert Ellis (1913–) and Aaron Beck (1921–). The distinctive aspect of their approach is the value they place on rationality as the most adaptive or healthy basis of behaviour, and the primacy of *thought* (and, to a lesser extent, action) over feelings and emotions. Bandura views *self-efficacy* – a belief in the self as competent to control the environment – as critical for good mental health. According to his theory, many mental-health problems result when people view themselves as passive victims of environmental events and forces.

Beck uses the findings of modern experimental psychology in his approach to the personality. Psychologists agree that there is so much potential information in the world around us that every experience would be novel and impossible to manage unless our minds imposed some sort of structure on it. This structure gives meaning to our experience and makes efficient use of our limited mental capacities. (For example, driving a well-practised route to work demands little of us because it matches up with a pre-existing set of mental expectations. We do not need to give it all our attention and are free to think of other things, such as the day ahead. But if road works necessitate a detour, we have to give our whole mind to the situation.)

We come to each new experience with a set of preconceptions about the way the world is that enable us both to make sense of it and to interact effectively with it. These preconceptions develop throughout childhood and are based on experience, but also, to a certain extent, constrain experience. In the area of visual perception this is well illustrated by the phenomenon of visual illusions. An example is provided by what is sometimes known as the 'Peter–Paul goblet' (figure 1.1).

Figure 1.1: The Peter–Paul goblet

This is usually perceived initially as a goblet. On looking at the illustration for longer, however, it begins to appear as the profile of two human faces. The two perceptions often alternate. The mind thus entertains two competing hypotheses about the meaning of the stimulus picture, but it cannot hold them both at the same time.

Thus individuals come to all events with preconceptions which influence their actual experience of the events. Beck describes the personality as a complex collection of assumptions about the world. Such a collection is termed a schema. Schemas can be thought of as core absolute beliefs acting as mental maps, which drive the way in which events are interpreted. Some of these may be explicit and freely expressed, such as 'All men are the same – they only want one thing!' However, many others may enter awareness only as the result of careful probing.

One important example of such a mental map is the *self-schema*. This is derived from the monitoring of the individual's own behaviour, his or her emotions, the judgments made by others, and a sense of belonging to a family or other social grouping. Once the self-schema begins to emerge in childhood, events are interpreted in such a way as to consolidate it as a permanent mental structure. *Self-evaluation* takes place through a series of appraisals, made with reference to other schemas concerned with aspirations and values. Beck describes the content of this self-evaluation as including judgments of personal worth, attractiveness, competence and ability to satisfy aspirations.

The self-evaluation is reflected in *underlying assumptions* and *automatic thoughts*. Underlying assumptions are conditional 'If ... then' beliefs: for instance, 'If I confide in people, then they will reject me', and are the pragmatic personal rules governing the everyday life of the individual. Automatic thoughts occur at times of stress and are habitual and often barely conscious: for instance, 'I am going to look stupid again.'

In many ways, Beck's account of self-evaluation is similar to that of Freud. In particular, both acknowledge a process of 'internalizing' the opinions of significant others in forming a view of the self. Freud's account is given in the language of the hydraulic scientific models of his day, whereas Beck's uses the language of information systems. Freud deals primarily with feelings, where Beck deals with thoughts. The accounts of Beck and other cognitive psychologists, while limited in some respects, provide a testable hypothesis about the way ideas about the self originate and are maintained. For this reason, these accounts have a better claim to scientific status that those of Freud.

Client-centred psychotherapy

An earlier development from ego psychology, which differs from cognitive psychology in important respects, is the client-centred humanistic approach of Carl Rogers (1902–87). For Rogers, the importance of self-acceptance to healthy personality function involves a relinquishing of the values of others in experiencing the self, and a discovery that the underlying self is both worthwhile and likeable. This account reflects Rogers's humanism – the view that being human is sufficient to merit worth and that all individuals are basically good when the external pressures and mental conflicts that cause selfish behaviour are removed. This contrasts sharply with Freud's more pessimistic account of the darker aspects of human nature.

Rogers holds that there is a superficial or false self that is experienced through the individual's habitual behaviour and in terms of the values of others. Behind this façade (which could be thought of as a defence) lies the real, true or deep self. The true self can be experienced only through an openness to raw feeling and may be accepted without the necessity of judging. Rogers was undoubtedly influenced by the writings of the Danish existentialist philosopher Søren Kierkegaard (1813–55). Kierkegaard described the process of *self-knowledge* as evolving and fluid. The true self is seen as 'becoming' or 'potential'. Both Rogers and Kierkegaard advocate self-knowledge and self-acceptance, but they deplore self-concern and self-preoccupation. Rogers thus introduces the idea of there being two selves to know, or two ways of experiencing the self. One is based largely on externals, and the other on the interior life. This idea owes something to Carl Jung (see next chapter).

Abraham Maslow (1908–70) advocates *self-actualization* as the basis for healthy personality function. In many ways, his position is similar to that of Rogers. Maslow made a distinctive and highly influential contribution to popular psychology by postulating a hierarchy of human needs. Maslow argues that the lower needs of human beings are basic to survival: food, drink, shelter and clothing. Next come psychological needs: a sense of belonging, friendship and *self-esteem*. The highest needs are described as spiritual: personal fulfilment, values and aesthetics. Higher needs cannot be fulfilled until the lower needs are met.

Although the term 'needs' has some unfortunate connotations (such as the idea of passively waiting for something or someone else to meet those needs, or the demanding and self-centred idea that needs must be met), it is clear that this model treats intact self-esteem as essential to all higher human activity. Self-esteem is viewed as a means to a better end.

This brief review should have made clear that the concept of self-esteem (even if it is not always called by this name) has been a central feature of many of the psychologies and psychotherapies of the last hundred years. It appears in many guises, each determined to a large extent by the philosophical and psychological orientation of the writer. The pervasiveness of the concept is one of its most interesting features, and it is tempting to conclude that this in itself signifies the existence of a real universal mental phenomenon, touched on in a slightly different way by each of the theories described above.

Self-esteem in historical and cultural context

However, a note of caution must be sounded. The preoccupation with self-awareness and self-discovery (which are the first steps in the process of self-evaluation) is largely a phenomenon of the recent past and the present. It should be noted that the experience and expression of the personal was very different, if not absent, in the Middle Ages (c. 700–1450).

In his study of the development of individual awareness, *Identity: Cultural Change and the Struggle for Self*, Roy F. Baumeister points to some major social trends that appeared around the dawn of the sixteenth century. Each trend reflected the new awareness of personal identity and distinctiveness. From these developments we gain a cumulative picture of an emerging new understanding of the self in western society. We consider three such developments to indicate the transition in western thinking that underlies the modern idea of 'self-esteem', and especially the importance attached to the subject by so many westerners.

First, a new concept of *a hidden or inner self* emerges, often centring on the observed discrepancy between outward behaviour and inner motivation. The idea of the self as an inner or hidden entity, not necessarily faithfully reflected in outward actions, began to develop. There was increasing realization that people might choose not to reveal their true selves by their outer actions. We see this particularly in the renewed interest in the idea of *hypocrisy*. Culturally, it means that people realized that the outward, observable actions of individuals were not necessarily a reliable guide to their true selves. The 'true self' began to be understood as an inward, almost secret entity that could not be fully known by outside observers.

In many ways, this idea can be regarded as a rediscovery of the scriptural distinction between the outward appearance and inward reality of people, evident in Jesus' criticism of hypocrites as 'whitewashed tombs' (Matt. 23:27–28). During the Middle Ages, it seems that the distinction between the inner and the outer self was neglected. Its rediscovery at the time of the Renaissance and Reformation made the New Testament come to life at point after point, including our understanding of self-esteem.

Secondly, people showed increasing interest in the idea of *individuality*. Cultural historians have suggested that the sixteenth century was an era in which 'people became individuals'. A new emphasis came to be placed upon the unique characteristics and identity of individuals. This development is linked with an explosive increase in the writing of autobiographies. The literary genre of autobiography reflects a heightened interest in and appreciation of the distinctive features of individuals' lives – features which might not necessarily be shared by others. The celebration of individuality points to an increasing belief that each person possessed a distinct and unique 'self', which was to be valued precisely on account of its uniqueness. The term 'self-praise' first makes its appearance in English in 1549, coinciding with this new valuation of the self – a crucial development, it will be appreciated, in relation to the question of self-esteem.

Thirdly, increasing value came to be placed upon *privacy*. In the Middle Ages, privacy was not regarded as important – a fact reflected in the design of houses, which made minimal, if any, allowance for privacy. Rooms were regarded as public spaces, not reserved for any individual or any particular function (such as sleeping or eating). The growing use of corridors in large houses dates from the early eighteenth century, when a growing desire for privacy led to allocating each guest or household member a room for his or her exclusive use. Roy Baumeister (1986: 24) comments on the significance of this development:

> Privacy is conceptually related to individuality, and it symbolizes the hidden self. Both privacy and individuality emphasize and strengthen the inner self by separating it from the broader network of society. The separation of public and private domains of life ... laid the foundation for a view of the self as being in conflict with society.

Other developments reinforce this impression of a new interest in and awareness of individual identity, a notion often explicitly stated in terms of 'the self'. For example, a new attitude developed towards death, reflecting an increased concern with individual fate. Whereas the Middle Ages tended to treat death in a fairly matter-of-fact manner, later periods became increasingly preoccupied with it, aware of the threat it posed to individual existence.

Nevertheless, this new awareness of individuality was not common to every social class. Even where the literature or culture of a society suggests a well-developed sense of individual identity in its intelligentsia, this is no guarantee that all sectors of that society share equal degrees of access to self-awareness. Introspection is something of a luxury, which would not necessarily be available to peasants and industrial workers living before the twentieth century. Their daily lives consisted largely of an unrelenting struggle to find the next meal and stay alive, in the context of a limited physical location and restricted set of relationships.

In more recent times, the depersonalizing nature of institutions (such as prisons, labour camps, or long-stay psychiatric hospitals) has been recognized. In his book *Asylums* (1968), Irving Goffman demonstrated how individual identity and self-awareness can be lost or totally fail to develop in such settings.

It seems that a self-concept can emerge only under certain favourable conditions: for example, time to observe oneself and a reasonably rich and varied context in which to do so. (Maslow's analysis is helpful in that it draws this point to our attention.) However, it seems highly likely that in some contemporary cultures the degree of individual self-awareness is limited or poorly articulated, although these conditions are met. This is most likely where strong identification with a family or tribe is seen as the norm, or where (as in animism) the boundaries between the human individual and the animal and plant environment are less clearly drawn than in the industrialized countries of the 'developed' world.

This illustrates the cultural relativism of all concepts relating to the self, and specifically to self-esteem. At the most obvious level, it is clear that the enhancement of self-esteem is of particular interest in North American culture. It is seen as a relatively less important issue in the traditionally more diffident and understated British culture, which considers self-deprecation a hallmark of civilized behaviour. At the furthest extreme stand traditional Chinese cultures, where self-abasement, to the degree of humiliation, is prized as a sign of great courtesy. Like many psychological concepts, self-esteem cannot be thought of as a uniform and universal aspect of human nature in the way that blood pressure or muscle strength can.

Yet, surprisingly, this is exactly the way self-esteem is treated by many writers and practising psychological therapists, who talk loosely about individuals 'not having sufficient self-esteem', or of 'having damaged self-esteem' (as if they had taken a precise reading of their blood-sugar level). There are no grounds for understanding self-esteem in this simplistic way. Indeed, it is seriously misleading to do so.

Psychological models

In all areas of study, the understanding of observed phenomena is assisted by the construction of models. As cognitive psychologists such as Beck have argued, it is likely that the mind has a natural propensity to construct such representations of experiences. Models help understanding, in the first place by organizing what might otherwise be a diffuse chaotic collection of data, and in the second by relating novel experience to what is already familiar. Freud's application of some of the laws of thermodynamics to the study of mental phenomena is a good example of this second use of a model. Jesus' use of examples from the world of agriculture to illustrate aspects of the kingdom of God is another example.

The value of a model depends upon the degree to which it makes complex phenomena understandable or, especially in science, the degree to which it generates novel creative hypotheses that can be tested. The appropriate question to ask when evaluating a model is not 'How similar to reality is it?' but 'How useful is it?' Models are better thought of as tools than as photographs. It is clear that Jesus was well aware of this distinction from his conversation with Nicodemus (John 3:1–21):

> ... Jesus declared, 'I tell you the truth, no-one can see the kingdom of God unless he is born again.'
>
> 'How can a man be born when he is old?' Nicodemus asked. 'Surely he cannot enter a second time into his mother's womb to be born!' ...
>
> 'You are Israel's teacher,' said Jesus, 'and do you not understand these things? I tell you the truth, we speak of what we know, and we testify to what we have seen ... I have spoken to you of earthly things and you do not believe; how then will you believe if I speak of heavenly things?' (John 3:3–4, 10–12).

In speaking of the need to be 'born again', Jesus was using the image of birth as a tool, a stimulus to reflection, rather than as a precise literal description of the process of renewal and regeneration necessary to enter the kingdom of God.

If the psychological theories presented earlier in this chapter are examined in the light of the above discussion, we see, first, that all are accounts of elaborate and complex models. That is, they are not literal representations of reality. Self-esteem occurs as a *construct*, a constituent part of these mental models.

Secondly, while many of these models are undoubtedly useful (in terms of aiding comprehension of mental phenomena), few of them can claim to be *scientific*. With the exception of the work of some of the cognitive behaviour therapists, the theories are not stated in ways that make them amenable to rigorous testing. There have been some experimental investigations into the efficacy of *therapies* based upon these theories; that, however, is not the same as an evaluation of the validity of the theories themselves.

We must always bear in mind the limitations of some psychological theories. A common tendency in popular literature is to make confident statements along the lines of 'Psychology has shown that ...' In fact, a more accurate statement would be, 'The psychological view of this is that ...' Where a psychological view has not been confirmed by experimental testing, it is unscientific. It thus has a status comparable to that of a religious viewpoint. It is quite inappropriate to treat it as if it had a different or higher status.

This is not to argue that self-esteem is a spurious or nonsensical concept. Rather, it is to ensure that its status is made clear and that it is not overvalued. To summarize: self-esteem is a *hypothetical construct of provisional and approximate nature*. Although there have been some empirical investigations of self-esteem, the models of which it forms a part are in general unscientific. It is culturally relative, but appears to be well represented in contemporary western psychologies. It is an attractive concept with good face value.

A definition of self-esteem

It is now time to draw together the arguments in this chapter to generate a definition of the hypothetical construct of self-esteem that will be used throughout this work.

Before doing this, two questions must be considered. First, is self-esteem global, referring to the whole person, or are there a series of discrete views of the self, specific to each area of life? And if the latter, how many views of the self are there? There is some evidence in favour of viewing the construct as global in nature. Questionnaires asking people to rate their self-esteem in one single global judgment correlate well with more detailed and extensive questionnaires that examine many different aspects of their lives.

Secondly, what relative emphasis should be given to the emotional and cognitive aspects of self-esteem? Is it primarily a feeling, or is it a judgment? The answer to this question is that the construct must incorporate both aspects, with the cognitive aspects perhaps being given priority. The evaluation precedes the feelings.

Therefore our working definition of self-esteem is as follows:

Self-esteem consists of a global evaluation or judgment about personal acceptability and worthiness to be loved, which carries with it pleasant or unpleasant feelings. It is strongly related to the perceived views of the person by important others in his or her life.

The relationship between self-esteem and other similar terms needs to be clarified. The following summary, based on material presented in this chapter, indicates the way self-esteem relates to other terms used in the literature on this subject.

- 'Self-regard' and 'self-worth' mean essentially the same as self-esteem.
- 'Self-schema', 'self-awareness', 'self-knowledge', 'self-appraisal' and 'self-concept' refer to the non-evaluative processes on which self-esteem is based.
- 'Self-reliance' and 'self-efficacy' refer to a constituent element of self-esteem, related to competence.
- 'Self-actualization' and 'self-acceptance' refer to hypothetical higher-order processes of which positive self-esteem is a necessary but not a sufficient part.

Having introduced the concept of self-esteem, our next task is to review what is known about the way it is maintained, details of its possible origins in childhood, and its role in mental health.

2

The basis of self-esteem

The previous chapter was concerned with descriptions and definitions of self-esteem in the context of a number of theories of the whole personality. In this chapter, we examine in more detail the content of self-esteem and the way in which self-esteem (either positive or negative) is maintained. That is, we have moved on from the question 'What is self-esteem?' to the question 'On what is self-esteem based?' In attempting to answer this question, we shall relate our account as much as possible to the results of empirical investigations.

Several empirical studies of self-esteem have been carried out since the 1960s. These have attempted to measure the concept using questionnaires. These questionnaires have generally contained items relating to the following key areas: *adequacy*, *worth*, *goodness* or *virtue*, *health*, *appearance*, *skills*, *sexuality*, *social competence* and *power*.

The judgment of self-esteem appears to draw from four main domains. These are *pedigree*, *performance of roles*, *the love of another* and *eternal significance*. These are not entirely independent of one another. Indeed, some sources of self-esteem – such as 'power' – can be thought of as straddling more than one domain.

Self-esteem and role

The first two domains – pedigree and performance – are both
closely linked with the concept of role. Put very simply, a role is the
part played by a person in a social system. The system can range in
size from two people to a whole nation. This notion is expressed
succinctly by Shakespeare:

All the world's a stage,
And all the men and women merely players:
They have their exits and their entrances;
And one man in his time plays many parts.
(*As You Like It*, Act II, Scene 7)

Despite the apparent simplicity of the concept, it is of great
significance in understanding human behaviour.

Any individual may hold a series of roles: parent, child, student,
professional, skilled amateur, patient, lover, friend, spouse and so
on. Each individual moves in and out of several roles each day.
Some sociologists have argued that it is possible to define an
individual exclusively in terms of the roles he or she assumes, and
some use the term 'social death' to refer to people deprived of these
social functions by extreme disability or incarceration in certain
types of institutions. For instance, Nazi concentration camps
aimed at the physical and personal destruction of the Jews and
other enemies of the Third Reich. The former was achieved
through the gas chambers, whereas the latter was accomplished by
eliminating all personal qualities and actions. Thus the inmates of
the prison camps were referred to by number, rather than by name,
and were prevented from exercising the normal social roles that
gave them a sense of personal identity and purpose.

The essential aspect of roles is their social nature. The individual's private plans and goals find their public expression in role
assumption. Roles give meaning to actions. The British sociologist
George Brown has argued that it is as one perceives oneself
successfully performing a role that the inner psychological and the
outer social worlds meet. Not only do individuals see themselves in
terms of roles, but they require others to enable the acting out of

these roles. They require a supporting cast. Thus while the individual sees others in terms of their roles, he or she sees them also in relation to the enactment of his or her own valued roles. For example, a woman might see her husband not only as 'spouse', 'lover' and 'parent'; she would also see him as the person who enables her to be 'wife'. Part of the pain of bereavement is the loss of role that goes along with the loss of a loved person – in this case, the change in status from 'wife' to 'widow'.

Self-esteem and pedigree

Pedigree can be thought of as the 'Who am I?' and 'Where did I come from?' aspect of a person's role. The importance of pedigree in establishing a feeling of belonging is well illustrated by the striving of new communities to find their roots. The history of the United States of America shows this up especially well. Ethnic groupings, faced with the threat of being overwhelmed by a larger, more amorphous culture, choose to resist this development. How? By asserting their distinctiveness. Irish-Americans, anxious to preserve their cultural identity, celebrate their Irish roots with a degree of commitment and enthusiasm that is always something of a mystery to those who chose to stay behind in Ireland. Many recent American presidents have found it to be electorally important to discover that they have links – however distant – with the Emerald Isle. St Patrick's Day is celebrated with far greater fervour in New York than it is in Dublin. Why? Because it preserves the identity of a group that would otherwise lose its distinctive character. The same is true of the American Jewish community, which finds in the Passover celebrations a focus for its sense of identity and continuing purpose.

Alex Haley's novel of the 1970s, *Roots*, made a deep and emotive appeal to this same sense of being rooted in the past. The new interest in the rediscovery of the African roots of black American culture is yet another illustration of this general principle of the importance of cultural roots, as is the rise of Rastafarianism (a religion that affirms the imperial African origins of Afro-Caribbeans) among such immigrants in England.

The recollection of past roots aids the preservation of present individuality. Where you come from says a lot about who you are. The current interest in genealogies also shows this concern to trace one's ancestors. On the individual level, it is generally recognized that children who have been separated from their natural families through adoption or disasters (such as wars) strive to find these lost families as soon as the opportunity presents itself.

Not only does a knowledge of pedigree go some way towards answering the question 'Who am I?', but it can also act as a means of enhancing self-esteem. The Old Testament writers traditionally use pedigree to validate the personal credentials of a particular character. The genealogies given at the beginning of Matthew (1:1–17) and Luke (3:23–38) present Jesus as a true Jew and a son of Adam. However, the most striking biblical use of pedigree as grounds for self-esteem is found in Paul's letter to the Philippians (3:4–5): 'If anyone else thinks he has reasons to put confidence in the flesh, I have more: circumcised on the eighth day, of the people of Israel, of the tribe of Benjamin, a Hebrew born of Hebrews ...'

In the secular world, pedigree is of similarly great importance. In Britain, a hereditary title preceding a person's name says much about that person and ensures deferential treatment from others. The United States also has its share of old-established families, as can be seen from the network of associations still carried by names such as Kennedy and from the importance of the idea of 'old money'. Our views of one another are highly coloured by the knowledge of the identity of parents and grandparents.

Perhaps the clearest example of this comes from the conversations of young children. They may boast, 'My daddy's bigger than your daddy', or 'My daddy's more important than yours.' A Freudian might interpret this sort of talk as reflecting identification with a parent. But we do not need such an elaborate interpretation to conclude that parental status can be invoked to enhance self-esteem.

In some societies, pedigree is of overriding importance in determining the worth of individuals. This is usually for reasons of maintaining racial purity, as in Nazi Germany or under the apartheid regime in South Africa. In such societies, the law ensures that family connections determine social rights.

Self-esteem and performance of roles

Performance of roles can be thought of as the 'What do I do?' aspect of a person's role. This area has been most extensively studied by experimental psychology and sociology. It is concerned with abilities and achievements and may be reflected in possessions or wealth. The archetypal presentation of the self in terms of achievement is the curriculum vitae or résumé. However, not all valued achievements occur in the context of paid employment. For instance, it would be possible to write an analogous list of life achievements for the full-time housewife or mother.

Research into children who suffer facial deformity has clearly demonstrated that the most significant predictor of good social and emotional adjustment in these children is the presence of a single valued skill or ability. It appears that if the child sees himself or herself as, for example, excelling at team sports, the emotionally damaging effects of the disfigurement are mitigated. There is a parallel effect in the peer group, which is more likely to accept the child if he or she can demonstrate a special skill.

Scripture also provides many examples of the importance of abilities, skills and behaviour in enhancing self-esteem. 'God, I thank you that I am not like other men – robbers, evildoers, adulterers – or even like this tax collector. I fast twice a week and give a tenth of all I get' (Luke 18:11–12). 'Lord, Lord, did we not prophesy in your name, and in your name drive out demons and perform many miracles?' (Matt. 7:22). St Paul continues his account of his personal credentials as a Jew prior to his conversion, speaking of his achievements in that capacity: 'as for zeal, persecuting the church; as for legalistic righteousness, faultless' (Phil. 3:6).

It is very important to understand that the relationship between actual behavioural achievements and adequate role assumption is not simple. For example, one woman's definition of an adequate housewife might entail her cleaning her kitchen floor every day; another woman might think that once a week is sufficient, where a third might regard floor-cleaning and homemaking as totally unconnected. Again, one student's criterion for success might be to obtain average marks of B+, whereas another might regard any mark under an A as failure. The same achievements may signify success for one person and failure for another. Thus the achievement criteria for adequate role assumption are subjective. They are also related to comparisons with others. If no-one in your neighbourhood cleans the kitchen floor every day, it is unlikely to be incorporated into your view of adequate homemaking; conversely, if all bake their own bread, this may become a significant component of your appraisal of your own homemaking capabilities.

People derive an enormous degree of pride and pleasure from the feeling that they have done a job well. This is true whether the job is leading a country, raising a family or painting the bathroom walls. Conversely, people experience distress and pain when they fail. However, individuals vary in two respects here: first, in their apparent degree of need to achieve, and secondly, in the particular areas of their life which they value most in this respect.

Investment in social roles

The need to achieve has been described in terms of *emotional investment* in particular roles. Where a person has invested highly, failure is devastating and success extremely rewarding. Part of the elation associated with success is that the devastation of failure has been avoided. Where the risks are especially great, success brings a considerable sense of achievement. Some individuals appear to invest more in role performance than others. For example, failing an examination might elicit a 'You win some, you lose some' response from one person, but might result in another's attempted suicide.

Individuals differ, often for cultural reasons, concerning the role or roles in which they choose to invest. One person may view his or her role as a sexual person as being of great significance, where another may be more interested in vocational success. Furthermore, some individuals tend to invest in a single role at the expense of all others, while others spread their investment more equitably; they choose not to put all their eggs in one basket. There is some evidence that over-investment in one role can lead to problems when the opportunity to assume this role is removed. For instance, a woman who has invested all her effort in motherhood may become extremely unhappy when her children leave home, just as a middle-aged man who has devoted his life exclusively to his career may find himself unable to cope well with redundancy. Losing something is more painful when there are no alternative sources of satisfaction available.

To summarize, people appear to vary with respect to their evaluation of role performance along three dimensions: first, the standards they set themselves; secondly, their overall amount of emotional investment in success; and thirdly, the way in which this investment is spread.

The persona

The work of Carl Jung (1875–1961) provides some interesting insights into the way performance of roles is related to self-esteem. Jung was originally a colleague of Freud, but later broke away from Freudian theories. Jung's theory of the personality describes a number of 'archetypes'. These can be thought of as predispositions to think and act in certain ways. One archetype is the persona. This is an inherited tendency to think and act in a conformist way that facilitates social acceptance and social integration.

The development of such a psychological predisposition makes sense in evolutionary terms. Stable social structures are likely to be maintained where individuals tend to conform. Social acceptance is seen to depend upon the individual's successful role assumption. Inadequate performance of role behaviours is seen as a threat to such acceptance within society. Thus striving for success is motivated both by fear of failure and by fear of consequent rejection.

The persona is, however, only one aspect of the self, and Jung argues that, if it becomes over-inflated, an unhealthy dependence upon achievement can result. To quote from a contemporary psychologist:

> This is the situation where an individual learns that the outward success of his persona is the means to personal happiness. The person can only be happy if the part he is playing (parent, lover, academic, sportsman, etc.) is acceptable, and is reinforced by others ... Failure must be avoided at all costs, for without the reinforcement of others, self-esteem is dealt a catastrophic blow (Gilbert 1992: 328).

This is a recurring theme in writings on the relationship between achievement and self-esteem: too strong a dependence upon external sources of reward (that is, over-investment in success) is thought to be psychologically unhealthy.

In his first-hand account of life in a concentration camp, the Jewish psychiatrist Bruno Bettelheim (1903–90) observed differences in the way that individuals coped with the intense pressures and stresses to which they were exposed. He contrasted the reactions of three groups: non-political, middle-class prisoners; common criminals; and political or religious 'conscientious' prisoners. He concluded that the criminals coped best, the 'conscientious' prisoners coped moderately well, and the non-political prisoners coped worst:

> No consistent philosophy, either moral, political or social, protected their integrity or gave them strength for an inner stand against Nazism. They had little or no resources to fall back on when subjected to the shock of imprisonment. Their self-esteem had rested on the status and respect that came with their positions, depended on their jobs, on being head of the family, or similar external factors ... Then all of a sudden everything that made them feel good about themselves for so long was knocked from under them (1960: 120–121).

Both Jung and Rogers have described role performance as a mask that does not truly reflect the real or whole self. Jung argues that only when a person relinquishes dependence on an omnicompetent persona (with the death of what he terms 'the hero ideal') can true personal development take place.

Thus the association between positive self-esteem and external achievement is not inevitable or straightforward, and may not even be desirable. The relationship is highly complex. It is not adequate simply to commend success and achievement as a means of enhancing self-esteem (as, for instance, Schuller 1982).

Self-esteem and the love of another

In describing the persona, we touched on the love of another as a source of self-esteem. Several components to self-esteem are more directly related to desirability and lovableness than to achievement. These are appearance, some aspects of sexuality, goodness, virtue and worth. Health may also reflect this domain; illness and disability can often bring rejection by others. Leprosy and Aids provide extreme examples. Perceiving oneself as being loved by another may mitigate the effects of failure.

One of the most popular series produced for American television is Matt Groening's *The Simpsons*. In part, its popularity is due to the way it perceptively addresses a whole series of issues relating to self-esteem, such as failure and underachievement. In one episode, Homer (Bart Simpson's father) undergoes a dramatic transformation when his baldness is cured. He acquires a new status within his corporation as he is upgraded to an executive position. Suddenly, his baldness returns – and his executive status vanishes. 'Never mind,' his wife tells him, 'we all love you anyway.' And they all live more or less happily thereafter.

Again, popular romantic fiction often describes the heroine being made to feel 'like a real woman' through the amorous attentions of the hero. In other words, her identity is achieved through being an object of love:

> She swallowed a little. 'I can't be one of your women, Marc ...'
>
> 'My women? Jan, darling ... none of them have meant even one tenth of what you mean!' His face was utterly serious now, his eyes as dark and soft as a dove's wing. 'I don't want you to be one of "my women", Jan – I want you to be my *woman* ...'

Achievements may be viewed as ways of earning love, as Jung has pointed out. However, the reverse is also the case. The fact that an individual has many friends, and is popular and socially successful, can itself be viewed as an achievement.

Thus being acceptable or loved and achieving success are closely and reciprocally related. This insight helps make sense of the tradition of presenting offerings to God, first seen in the Old Testament in the story of Cain and Abel, who each offered a prime representative sample of their labours to God, with the clear objective of achieving personal acceptability in his sight (Gen. 4:1–7).

Self-esteem and eternal significance

The desire for *eternal significance* is reflected in people's pre-occupation with immortality and with their relatively tiny size in a vast universe. They may strive to make their mark on the world, to produce descendants, or to live for as long as possible. The title song of the 1980s television series 'FAME!', based on the aspirations of a group of performing-arts students, included the deeply revealing words, 'I want to live for ever!' and 'Remember my name!' This striving seems to be an attempt to protect the self from feelings of eternal aloneness and alienation, perhaps springing from an acknowledgment that achievements and the approval of others are fragile and short-lived sources of self-esteem. The writer of Ecclesiastes anticipated this point:

> Generations come and generations go,
> but the earth remains for ever (1:4).

Man's fate is like that of the animals; the same fate awaits them both: As one dies, so dies the other … All go to the same place; all come from dust, and to dust all return (3:19–20).

In his poem 'Ozymandias', Percy Bysshe Shelley explores this quest for permanence. He tells of a monument in an ancient land:

> I met a traveller from an antique land
> Who said: Two vast and trunkless legs of stone
> Stand in the desert.

This ruined monument turns out to be all that remains of a tribute to the power of a long-dead king:

> 'My name is Ozymandias, king of kings:
> Look on my works, ye Mighty, and despair!'

The monument proclaims this king's self-esteem. He will be remembered in history on account of his great works. Yet nothing remains of these works. The words ring empty. The monument is a sad testimony to past glory and present ruin, decay and insignificance:

> Nothing beside remains. Round the decay
> Of that colossal wreck, boundless and bare
> The lone and level sands stretch far away.

Not only is humanity's temporal span brief, but we are just tiny specks on a planet in one of millions of galaxies in an expanding universe. This is an existentially challenging fact, calling up deep anxieties. Most people cope with it by ignoring it most of the time, but it is also reflected in both mainstream scientific and populist preoccupations with life on other planets. Humankind's apparent cosmic insignificance was well summed up over two thousand years ago by the psalmist:

> When I consider your heavens,
>   the work of your fingers,
> the moon and the stars,
>   which you have set in place,
> what is man that you are mindful of him,
>   the son of man that you care for him?
>
> (Ps. 8:3–4)

Isaiah expresses the same thought, stressing the puny nature of humanity in comparison with the immensity of creation and its Creator:

> He sits enthroned above the circle of the earth,
>   and its people are like grasshoppers.
> He stretches out the heavens like a canopy,
>   and spreads them out like a tent to live in.
>
> (Is. 40:22)

The definition of self-esteem given at the end of the previous chapter incorporates the idea of personal acceptability. When individuals think of this in terms of their eternal significance, they are moving beyond wanting to be acceptable to a small circle of people here and now, and are searching for an *absolute* and unchanging standard of acceptability. For those who believe in God, this search may incorporate the more personal absolute standard of being worthy of being *loved* by an eternal Other.

Self-esteem and the interpretation of experience

So far, we have been examining the possible sources of self-esteem mainly in terms of events external to the person. As we have seen, these events may involve achievements by that person or the actions of others directed towards that person. They also involve objective facts, such as the person's family name or general human mortality. It is now necessary to go beyond the simple experience of these externals to examine the *interpretations* different people place upon their experience. As we have already described, individuals vary in the degree to which they rely upon role performance as a source of self-esteem and in relation to the particular roles in which they invest. However, they also vary in the way they interpret particular events as evidence that they have or have not performed adequately in a particular role. That is to say, they vary in their style of *causal attribution*.

The British empiricist tradition, especially the philosophy of David Hume (1711–76), has been highly influential in the development of experimental psychology. One key argument is that in everyday life causes are inferred by the observer in order to make sense of the relationship between events. Hume argued that the idea of a 'cause' arises in the following way. The observer notes that two events occur closely together in time and that one always precedes the other, and the second event never occurs unless the first event has preceded it. The observer concludes that the first event 'causes' the second. However, the first event may merely be a signal for the second event (as in traffic lights) or be associated with it by chance. In other words, the idea of a cause is something imposed by the observer upon the events, rather than a relationship inherent in the events. It is a human mental construct.

There is good evidence that individuals tend to assign causes according to their own particular style. For example, a middle-aged woman known to us, who failed her driving test five times, attributed this failure to a particular examiner's preference for 'sweet young girls', and not to any lack of driving skill on her part. The fact is uncontestable – she has been examined by this particular examiner and failed her driving test five times. But why? To what cause can this series of events be attributed? The woman, in attributing the cause to the examiner's preference for young girls, is locating the reason for her failure outside herself. As a result, she persevered and passed at the sixth attempt. But had she adopted an internal attributional style, putting her failure down to a total lack of driving skills, she might well have given up.

A friend of the family, aged eleven, who has never yet won a competition, attributed this to his being intrinsically unsuccessful: 'My life will never amount to anything.' He located the reason for his failure firmly inside himself, whereas actually he had just been unlucky.

Attributions vary along three main dimensions: *internal–external*, *stable–unstable* and *global–specific*. We shall explore each of these in turn.

Internal–external

This distinction centres on whether an event is attributed to causes internal or external to the person involved. For example, consider a student who has just been ditched by his girlfriend. He could attribute the breakup to internal factors (in other words, his girlfriend ended her relationship with him on account of something to do with him) or to external factors (she finished with him on account of some aspect of her nature). Consider these statements:

'My girlfriend broke up with me because I am unattractive.'

'My girlfriend broke up with me because she was unable to appreciate my good points.'

The first approach attributes the failed relationship to a deficiency in the student; the second to a shortcoming in his girlfriend.

Stable–unstable

This distinction hinges upon whether an event is attributed to something permanent and stable or to something transient and unstable. For example, consider the case of a student who has failed an important examination. Two possible attributions might be:

'I failed the examination because I *am* stupid.'

'I failed the examination because I *had* a migraine.'

In the first case, the failure is attributed to a permanent and stable feature of the student's life. She failed because she is stupid – and she will remain stupid. In the second case, failure is attributed to something transient – a migraine. No statement is being made about the student's permanent or stable abilities; the failure is due to a temporary set of circumstances, which had an adverse effect upon her performance.

Global–specific

This distinction centres upon whether it is the person considered as a totality who is responsible for an event or whether it is only one particular aspect of the person. For example, consider these two statements:

'I failed my maths test because I am *stupid.*'

'I failed my maths test because I am *no good at maths.*'

The first approach attributes the failure to a global feature of the person, the second to one specific inability. Much the same distinction arises in the following example, in which the first global attribution contrasts sharply with the second specific attribution:

'I look awful in photographs because I am *ugly.*'

'I look awful in photographs because I am *not photogenic.*'

An internal global attributional style lays the responsibility for events firmly within the person. If the individual also tends to make stable attributions (e.g. 'I am stupid'), little future change can be expected. If I think that I have failed an examination because I am stupid, my emotional reaction will be different from that of someone who thinks that she failed because the examination was too difficult, or was in a subject in which she never excelled, or because she was ill at the time. I would be likely to put less effort into retaking the examination, or would not bother to retake it at all.

Many writers have suggested that an internal attributional style with respect to failure is crucial in the maintenance of negative self-esteem. There is some evidence for this. Studies of children have shown that those scoring highly on self-esteem questionnaires are more likely to attribute success internally to their own abilities, whereas children with low scores tend to attribute success to external or unstable causes (e.g. 'luck'), but attribute failure internally (e.g. 'stupidity'). Children with low self-esteem scores do not expect to succeed, and any experiences of success can always be dismissed by them as insignificant, and as due to external factors rather than to their own abilities. These attributional styles can, and often do, persist into adulthood.

It is possible to manipulate self-esteem experimentally. Suppose subjects are presented with a task designed in such a way that it is impossible for anyone to succeed. When they duly fail to perform the task, they are then told that everyone else succeeded. As a result, their self-esteem (as measured on a rating-scale) drops. If instead they are told that everyone else failed, their self-esteem remains stable, unaffected by their failure at this task. In the former situation, a process of internal attribution takes place: the subjects believe that failure resulted from some deficiency on their part, on account of their belief that everyone else succeeded in the task. In the second instance, a process of external attribution takes place: as everyone failed, the explanation can only be the difficulty of the task. In other words, the problem lies outside the person.

It therefore seems that positive self-esteem may be maintained by a selective attribution of success to the self and of failure to externals, as in the case of the learner driver mentioned earlier. (In terms of some of the theoretical approaches reviewed in chapter 1, this attributional style can also be seen as a type of psychoanalytical defence, a cognitive coping strategy or the operation of an underlying assumption.) However, it is not clear that the relationship between self-esteem and attributional style is only one-way. Internal, global, stable attributions may maintain low self-esteem; but equally, low self-esteem may engender these styles of attribution. It is probably most helpful to view the whole situation as a vicious circle, with low self-esteem leading to certain attributions, and these in turn feeding low self-esteem:

'I never succeed because I am stupid' ⟷ 'I must be stupid

because I never succeed.'

Most of the examples discussed so far have related to role per-formance or achievement. Attributions are also made in the other domains that form the source of self-esteem, especially our worthi-ness to be loved by another. The unfriendly behaviour of others is easier to cope with if it can be attributed to a problem with them rather than with us. Conversely, someone's loving behaviour can be dismissed as an indiscriminate charitable attitude that person has towards *everyone* if the recipient feels unworthy of that love.

In summary, self-esteem seems to be based on the way we see ourselves in terms of our pedigree and background, our achieve-ments, our cosmic or eternal significance, and the extent to which we are loved by others. A particular view of the self will be main-tained by the attribution that we place on events. This attributional style may in its turn arise from the way we see ourselves.

One point remains to be considered. Attributional style is signi-ficant in relationship to self-esteem only where the inferred causes refer to cherished aspirations and/or moral values (see p. 47). Thus, the important question is not simply 'Did I cause that?' (physically) but 'Was that my fault?' (morally).

An example from the experience of one of the authors may clarify this distinction. When driving recently, I knocked a cyclist off her bicycle, causing her some minor injuries. She had cycled at speed on to a major road from a minor road without ensuring that it was safe to do so. As a result, she collided with the front of my car. I caused her injuries, but I had not acted negligently. I could not have swerved safely, and I was not speeding. I was sorry for her, but I felt no loss of self-esteem. This is in contrast to my feelings following a near miss when I overtook a bus without checking properly to ensure that it was safe to do so. No-one was hurt, but I had transgressed my own rules of competent driving. I blamed myself.

Here we see that one of the negative feelings which may accompany low self-esteem is guilt or self-blame. In extreme cases a person may see himself or herself as not only worthless, but as also deserving of punishment. This theme will be explored in more detail in the discussion of depression in the next chapter.

3

The function of self-esteem

In the previous chapters, we have tried to give an account of what self-esteem *is*, and of the ways it is fed or maintained, so that a particular view of the self is sustained. We now turn to the question of what self-esteem *does*. What function does it fulfil? What significance does self-esteem have for psychological well-being and for good personality function?

To address such questions, it is useful to look at the way self-esteem ('measured' by questionnaires, rating-scales and interviews) relates to other independent measures of psychological well-being or mental health. In doing this, it must be remembered that the fact that one observation is found to be associated with another does not prove that the one causes the other. For example, if it were shown that negative self-esteem is associated with mental-health problems, it would be premature to assume that such negative self-esteem causes those problems. The relation between them can be more complicated. The fact that A and B are associated with each other does not necessarily mean that A causes B or that B causes A. Both A and B might be the result of a third factor, C. Thus the observation that negative self-esteem and mental-health problems are associated could be interpreted in at least three different ways:

1. Negative self-esteem causes mental-health problems.
2. Mental-health problems cause negative self-esteem.
3. Negative self-esteem and mental-health problems are both caused by something else.

The process of assigning causation, and thus constructing explanations, in science is essentially identical to that of normal human psychology discussed in chapter 2. However, scientific approaches are based on a larger number of systematic observations under controlled conditions and, crucially, active experimentation. For instance, while the general statistical association between lung cancer and smoking was known for many years, the specific causal role played by inhalation of tobacco smoke was assigned only relatively recently as a result of well-contolled epidemiological studies and laboratory experiments.

We must therefore avoid jumping to a hasty conclusion that self-esteem has a causal role in personality function or in mental health. Keeping this important point in mind, we may turn to consider the evidence concerning self-esteem and other psychological measures.

As was noted in chapter 1, several psychotherapists (such as Adler, Horney and Rogers) are committed to the idea that positive self-esteem is a necessary prerequisite for the ability to interact effectively with others. This is because individuals with good self-esteem, it is believed, need not use others to bolster a positive image of themselves, nor do they perceive others as threats to their self-esteem; their behaviour is not motivated by fear.

Thus one would expect an association between positive self-esteem and assertive behaviour, and this is exactly what has been found. (*Assertiveness* should not be confused with *aggressiveness*. Assertive people are prepared to stand up for themselves or their beliefs, but not at the cost of offending or exploiting others.) Positive self-esteem is also reported to be associated with good physical health, satisfying relationships, the ability to tolerate and accept others, and hope for the future.

It has been shown that children with negative self-esteem tend to put less effort into their endeavours because they seem to have lowered expectations of success. This then becomes a self-fulfilling prophecy, which reinforces both the negative self-esteem and the low expectations of success. In adults, negative self-esteem has been shown to be associated with poor general health, over-submissiveness, passivity and compliance, a tendency to accept unfavourable assessments as accurate, poor scholastic and vocational success, and a tendency to denigrate others.

It may seem surprising that a person with negative self-esteem (conventionally thought of as being maintained by *internal* attributions) should denigrate others. It is probably helpful to think of such individuals as having *fragile* or *vulnerable* self-esteem, rather than *low* self-esteem. As a result, they make desperate attempts to preserve their self-esteem by continually comparing themselves favourably with others. This strategy can be thought of as a compensatory form of defence, and Adler makes much of it in his account of the inferiority complex.

Thus at least two abnormalities in self-esteem can lead to personal problems: naked, undefended poor self-esteem, and threatened, vulnerable self-esteem with its consequent maladaptive defences. In extreme cases, these characteristics of the personality can come to dominate it at the expense of all others. If this happens, the individual is described as suffering from a *personality disorder*. The lives of such individuals are full of problems in the interpersonal realm, and they are usually deeply dissatisfied.

Personality disorders

Nine types of personality disorder are described by the *Diagnostic and Statistical Manual* of the American Psychiatric Association. Abnormalities of self-esteem are not the main significant characteristics of all nine of these, though they feature incidentally to varying degrees. This is in itself an important observation, as it suggests that self-esteem cannot be used to explain every aspect of personal life and human pain. Curing abnormal self-esteem is therefore not some kind of panacea that will achieve psychological health in every situation – an assumption that seems to underlie Robert Schuller's *Self-Esteem: The New Reformation* (1982).

Nevertheless, two of the nine types of personality disorder do relate centrally to self-esteem. These are *avoidant personality disorder* and *narcissistic personality disorder.*

Avoidant personality disorder

The avoidant personality clearly suffers from chronic extreme low self-esteem. Such persons feel socially inept and generally incompetent and find criticism and rejection almost impossible to cope with. They tend to see other people as superior and potentially critical of them. If others appear to be positive and accepting, the avoidant personality usually thinks, 'They don't know the real me.' Such people avoid challenging social situations of any sort. They may have few relationships; what relationships they do possess are likely to be characterized by anxiety about potential rejection.

Narcissistic personality disorder

The narcissistic personality is, on the face of it, the direct opposite of the avoidant personality. Such a person feels special, unique and superior. He or she tends to see other people as inferior or potential admirers. Such a person assumes that he or she is entitled to the best, is above rules, and has the right to use other people to achieve his or her own ends. Perhaps the most characteristic feature of this personality disorder is the tendency to treat other people as objects. For example, if a friend has to cancel a date due to illness, the narcissistic person will be annoyed rather than sympathetic. Paradoxically, individuals suffering from narcissistic personality disorder are often unhappy and discontented and frequently seek psychiatric help.

It is possible to explain a narcissistic personality in two ways (indeed, there may be two possible routes to the same end phenomenon). First, it may be seen as an extreme defence of the sort of fragile self-esteem described above. Alternatively, it may be seen as naked, undefended, abnormally positive self-esteem. Freud and others have suggested that an abnormally approving view of the self arises from parental overvaluing of the child (although evidence for this suggestion is scanty).

In conclusion, reasonably convincing evidence shows an

association between high or positive self-esteem and adequate personality functioning on the one hand; and between low or negative self-esteem (and possibly extremely positive self-esteem) and poor personality function.

It is now necessary to examine evidence concerning mental illness.

Mental illness

The borderline between personality disorder and mental illness is not always clear. Where does eccentricity become madness? Indeed, many writers, such as Thomas Szass and Ronald D. Laing, have questioned the usefulness of describing psychological pain in terms of illness (the 'medical model') in the first place. The debate over the limitations of the medical model in psychiatry is beyond the scope of this book. For our purposes, while acknowledging its limitations, the use of a system of diagnostic categories of mental illness is accepted as a helpful approach.

The things that distinguish mental illness from personality disorder are

- the degree of distress it causes the sufferer
- a feeling that the sufferer is not his or her usual self (hence the idea of 'illness')
- a component of losing touch with reality

Poor personality function seems to make the individual vulnerable to mental illness. Some writers have described the situation in these terms. Mental illness can be thought of as a response to stress (either psychological or biological). For the vulnerable individual, only a small amount of stress can result in mental illness. However, as John Bowlby puts it, no person is invulnerable to every possible adversity. Thus even the most well-balanced person can be pushed to breaking-point by severe trauma. It is therefore possible to observe mental illness in the context of previously good personality function, or, as is often the case, in combination with long-standing personality disorder.

Anxiety disorders

Anxiety is an experience of everyday life which, like pain, is highly useful in helping the individual to interact effectively with the environment. It motivates our response to danger. Anxiety can be described as an emotional state which is subjectively experienced as a quality of fear. There are also associated physical symptoms, such as sweating, palpitations, dry mouth and, if the anxiety is caused by a specific stimulus, a strong desire to escape or avoid the situation.

Anxiety-related disorders are fairly common in the population. Approximately 10% of adults may be suffering in this way at any one time. Anxiety can be considered a disorder when the intensity and duration of the emotional response are out of all proportion to the perceived threat, and/or where elaborate avoidance strategies have been brought into play so that the person's life becomes restricted. An example of this is the agoraphobic person who is afraid to leave his or her home and depends entirely on others for shopping. Such a person has an impoverished social and vocational life. Another example is the spider phobic who takes two hours to get ready for bed at night because every square centimetre of the house has to be checked for lurking spiders.

The central theme in anxiety is *threat*. The threat may be physical – illness, injury, violation or death. The physical symptoms of anxiety mimic cardiac illness and can themselves be terrifying. However, anxiety can equally reflect psychosocial threats such as appearing foolish, being rejected or going mad. Thus some anxiety disorders, such as fear of public speaking, clearly reflect a threat to self-esteem.

Chronic worry and anxiety are future-orientated emotions. The anxious person may lie awake at night turning over a series of possible future scenarios in his or her mind. The catastrophic consequences of the feared events will be dwelt upon in thoughts such as 'It will be devastating if I stammer in my graduation speech.' These thoughts tend to centre around ideas of being accepted by others, being responsible for events and being competent. (The preoccupation with acceptance and competence clearly relates to self-esteem, as it was presented in chapter 2. The preoccupation with responsibility relates to an inability to trust others.) At other times, such people will be hyper-vigilant, or over-alert, to possible threats in the environment – seeing rejection when it is not there, or mistaking tomato calyces for spiders.

Anxiety disorders can be crippling in their consequences. Anxious people are often so involved in *self-preservation* and avoidance of threat that they are unable to develop as people and deal effectively with the needs of others. William James was troubled by a mysterious fear of ill health towards the end of his life. He was the first to admit that it turned him into a self-absorbed and selfish person. In anxiety disorders, personal identity, existence and self-esteem have become vulnerable, and the environment comes to be perceived as essentially hostile.

This resonates with some important scriptural insights. It is only when Adam and Eve sin that fear enters the world (Gen. 3:10). Similarly, the Gospels note how fear is abolished by trust in Christ (Matt. 14:28–33). It is only through the love of God that human fear can be cast out (1 John 4:18–19).

Paranoid delusions

One symptom of severe mental illness is the paranoid delusion. This usually occurs in the context of certain types of schizophrenia, but it can also be induced by drug or alcohol abuse. These delusions are beliefs – rigidly held, often elaborate, striking in their improbability and resistant to argument – that others are planning to harm the person: for example, that the secret police are spying on every action using cameras and bugging devices hidden in the home, and that the family doctor and others are in league with them. It is likely that these delusions represent attempts by the mind to make sense of the terrifying emotional changes and problems in perception and attention that the individual experiences as part of the illness. In more personal terms, paranoid delusions have been described as an elaborate defensive structure to preserve *self-esteem* in the face of the threat of disintegration of the personality.

The delusions are thus seen as extreme external attributions of negative events. This is a plausible hypothesis, and it fits with the experience of one of the authors.

My office is very untidy, with files and equipment strewn all over the place. However, I pride myself on always knowing where every item is. There is order among chaos. But recently several important items went missing. Two alternative interpretations presented themselves to me:

'I am hopelessly disorganized and incompetent.'

'Someone is *taking* things from my office on purpose.'

I chose the latter interpretation, presumably because the idea that I am incompetent is distasteful to me. Later I was ashamed to find all the missing items in places where I had obviously left them and forgotten! I was able to abandon my paranoid hypothesis in the face of the evidence. A paranoid delusion would not be so easy to modify, perhaps because the personal cost to self-esteem of laying it aside would be too great.

Both anxiety-related disorders and paranoid delusions can be seen as related to threatened self-esteem (although the perceived threat in both these conditions will refer to many other aspects of the person also). There is, however, one condition where the threat to self-esteem is realized and where pathologically negative self-esteem is a core defining feature. This condition is *depression*.

Depression

Everyone knows what it is like to feel sad or depressed. Clinical depression is qualitatively similar to this feeling, but it can reach crippling degrees of severity. It is a common condition, affecting 15% to 20% of the adult population at any one time. (A powerful and evocative picture of the psychological pain involved is given in Psalm 38, which is recommended for close study in its entirety at this point.)

There are several categories of depressive illness. All, however, have the same common features. A person suffering from depression may experience sadness, guilt, shame, anxiety, hopelessness, and even anger. There is likely to be sleep disturbance, loss of appetite and loss of sexual desire. Memory, concentration and thinking may be affected. Ordinary everyday tasks may become completely overwhelming, so that activity levels and the amount of social interaction drop dramatically. The depressed person may spend all day sitting in a chair, weeping, indifferent to personal appearance, nourishment or social duties. In many cases suicide will be contemplated and, in some cases, carried out. Without doubt, chemical changes take place in the brain during such depressive episodes. Depression is amenable to treatment by a range of medications. However, the accounts considered here are psychological rather than biological.

In recent years, much attention has been paid to the thought processes of depressed people. It has been pointed out that while anxiety is a future-orientated emotion ('What if?'), depression is very much concerned with what has happened in the past. In his *Mourning and Melancholia*, Freud drew attention to the fact that *loss* is a central theme in depression, noting similarities between depressed and bereaved individuals. The similarities between bereavement and depression are uncanny, even extending down to the details of the type of sleep disturbance involved.

There is, however, an obvious difference. While bereavement is a response to a clear significant loss, the origins of depression are more obscure. Whereas in bereavement, something has been lost *outside* the affected person, Freud suggested that in depression something *inside* the person has become lost or diminished – the ego. This ego loss can be identified with current descriptions of negative self-esteem, and Freud used it to explain the fact that while a very negative view of the self is characteristic of depression, it is not such a marked feature of bereavement.

Beck has described the core beliefs of the depressed person in terms of the following negative triad:

- the self as worthless
- the outer world as meaningless
- the future as hopeless

These beliefs reflect the appraisal of loss of the essential aspects of each of the three domains involved. Hatred of self accompanies depression. Depressed people may feel that they deserve to be punished for numerous sins, that others would be better off without them, and that they should terminate their own existence.

This hatred of self often centres around feelings of failure and rejection.

On the face of it, it seems likely that a person with the avoidant personality (that is, with ongoing negative self-esteem) would be prone to depression. Indeed, many writers have suggested that, given a particular stressful event, low self-esteem will increase the chance of a general appraisal of hopelessness. Beck argues that the negative triad of beliefs is lurking in a latent state in the depression-prone adult. There is evidence that self-esteem predicts the course and prognosis of depression, with very poor self-esteem being characteristic of a depression more resistant to treatment. The question of whether negative self-esteem actually makes people more vulnerable to the onset of depression in the first place remains controversial.

The cognitive-behavioural approach to depression

As described in chapter 1, the cognitive behaviour therapists, most notably Beck, give priority to *thoughts*. They direct therapy for depression towards changing automatic thoughts, and through these towards modifying the underlying dysfunctional (unhelpful) beliefs and schemas. The approach is collaborative; the therapist and client work as a team, and the client is encouraged to discover truths for himself or herself. Nevertheless, cognitive behaviour therapy is highly structured and subtly directive.

Cognitive behaviour therapy is highly effective in the treatment of depression, and it has been shown to have at least a short-term effect specifically on self-esteem. The cognitive model of low self-esteem describes a vicious circle in which a global negative judgment about the self leads to negative predictions about the future. For this reason, situations that could possibly be rewarding are avoided and any evidence of personal competence is discounted. Thus the negative judgment is confirmed and maintained.

Depressive automatic thoughts are held to be distorted and illogical, not only in their pattern of attribution (failures being attributed internally and successes being attributed externally), but also in the following ways:

Arbitrary inference: the tendency to draw a negative conclusion in the absence of supporting data (for example: 'It is a *fact* – *I* am no good').

Selective abstraction: focusing on a trivial detail out of context (for example: 'Although the meal I prepared was a success, the coffee was too weak, so the whole thing was a disaster').

Over-generalization: drawing conclusions for a wide variety of things on the basis of single events (for example: 'The supermarket checkout girl was rude to me today – therefore nobody likes me').

Magnification and minimization: making errors in evaluating the importance of events (for example: 'My boyfriend didn't phone me today – therefore he doesn't love me any more').

Absolutist dichotomous thinking: a way of thinking in black and white, which refuses to acknowledge the existence of intermediates (for example: 'Either you love me or you hate me').

The schemas (core beliefs) and underlying assumptions which are maintained by and which drive these distorted thought patterns are similarly held to be irrational. Examples of such core beliefs would be:

'It is essential for me to be liked by everybody' (core belief). Therefore, 'If I am not loved, I cannot be happy' (underlying assumption).

'To be acceptable, I must be perfect' (core belief). Therefore, 'If I fail at any task, I am worthless' (underlying assumption).

The reader may question whether such beliefs really are irrational, unhelpful or untrue. We shall return to this point in the next chapter.

The cognitive behaviour therapist challenges the automatic thoughts by asking the client to re-examine the evidence for his or her conclusions in a rational way and to generate alternative ways of interpreting the facts that gave rise to these thoughts in the first place. For example: 'The supermarket checkout girl might have been rude because she was suffering from indigestion, and she is, after all, only one person, whom I hardly know.' The client is set tasks in which his or her conclusions are tested out. For example, she might be invited to phone her boyfriend and find out why he didn't phone her the other night.

The underlying beliefs are also challenged using a variety of techniques and are evaluated explicitly in terms of how *helpful* or *advantageous* they are (rather than in terms of their absolute validity). For example, looking for someone to blame in a situation may not be helpful, and questions of moral responsibility are actively avoided. The client is encouraged to set lower realistic, attainable standards for him or herself and to stop striving for perfection. In particular, the consequences of certain facts are examined. 'If I fail at some of my endeavours, or if I am not loved by certain people, is that *really* so bad?'

The well-evaluated and good outcome of the cognitive behavioural approach demonstrates that changing the way people think about themselves, the world and the future can bring about recovery from a depressive episode. Yet, as freely acknowledged by most cognitive therapists, the cause of depression is not simply a particular cognitive style. Depression occurs in response to events in people's lives. In 1978 George Brown (a sociologist) and Tirill Harris (a psychiatrist) published a major study into the social origins of depression in urban British working-class women. This study showed that certain life events were associated with the development of clinical depression in these women. The events posed long-term threats or involved severe disappointment. Examples are the illness or death of a loved one; a major negative revelation about a close friend or relative; a threatened or actual job loss by self or spouse; and the necessity of moving from one home to another.

Notice that all of these events involve actual or potential long-term loss of something or someone precious.

However, the events led to depression in only some women. The women most vulnerable to depression following negative life events were those who had lost their mothers before the age of eleven; had a low degree of intimacy with their husbands; or had three or more children under the age of fourteen living at home, and no outside employment.

A combination of two or more of these three factors increased vulnerability to depression dramatically. The severity of the depression was related to the history of previous losses and separations, and to past psychiatric history in general.

Brown and Harris speculate that the vulnerability factors are linked by the concept of low self-esteem. A woman who had lost her mother or who experienced lack of intimacy with her husband might feel rejected. Being isolated at home in the under-recognized role of 'housewife' might lead to a negative self-evaluation. Thus while a particular type of thinking can maintain the impoverished self-esteem found in depression, significant life events and environmental factors also seem to have a powerful influence.

It is now possible to draw some conclusions about the role of self-esteem in relation to mental health. Without doubt, low self-esteem is strongly associated with, if not characteristic of, depression. Threatened self-esteem apparently plays a part in anxiety disorders, and it may be important in the generation of some symptoms of schizophrenia. There is increasing awareness of the role of self-esteem as a contributor to the maintenance of eating disorders such as anorexia nervosa and bulimia. Lastly, the rare condition of mania is characterized by an exhilarated and triumphant view of the self: 'I can do *anything*!' It seems that a *good*, but not *exaggerated*, judgment of the self is the hallmark of adequate personal function. In addition, this good judgment should not be too dependent upon external achievements or on the approval of others. In other words, it has to be robust as well as positive. In order to value others, it seems that one must first value oneself.

Why might this be so? What does good self-esteem protect the person from? When the cognitive behaviour therapist asks if it is really so bad to be rejected or to fail, the answer that comes naturally to our lips is, 'Yes, it is!' And this raises the question: Why?

Separation and self-esteem

One of the most striking findings of the study of Brown and Harris is the increased risk of depression in the case of women who had lost their own mothers (through either death or separation) before the age of eleven. Of all the vulnerability factors, this is the most historically distant. Its relationship to lowered self-esteem is not immediately obvious. To explore the significance of this study and what its implications for Christian self-esteem might be, we turn to the work of John Bowlby (1907–90), a British psychiatrist of psychodynamic orientation who undertook pioneering work on parent–child relations shortly after the end of the Second World War.

Bowlby was interested in the effects of temporary separation of the small child from his or her mother, usually during hospitalization. He noted a general pattern of behaviour, which was particularly marked in the case of children between the ages of six months and three years, but which extended beyond this age range. The separated children passed through three stages:

Protest. The child cries or calls for the mother, running after her or searching for her, and sometimes expressing anger. Anyone who has tried to leave an unwilling child in a crèche or in daycare will be familiar with this behaviour. Our daughter used to hold on silently to the hem of Joanna's full, rather long skirts as she tried to leave her, so that Joanna was literally pulled back into the room.

Despair. Here the child is in extreme distress, is inconsolable by others, and sobs in anguish.

Detachment. In this final stage, the child appears to realize that the mother is not going to return. He or she withdraws into the self, shows no interest in the surroundings and no willingness to interact with others. He or she may reject the mother when they are finally reunited.

This early work drew attention to the unnecessary suffering resulting from such separation and revolutionized childcare practices so that hospitals began to allow increased access to parents and eventually to provide facilities for parents to stay with their children when the children were hospitalized. It also generated a rather unhelpful argument about the possible detrimental effect on children when mothers take employment outside the home. (In fact, it is not just separation from mother that is so distressing for young children. Separation from other familiar adults and brothers and sisters has similar effects. In adolescence, separation from a peer group could be considered to be of similar significance.)

Why should separation from the mother be so extremely anxiety-promoting for young children? Bowlby answers this question by appealing to ethological work (careful naturalistic observations) on the behaviour or birds, mammals and humans. It had been argued for many years that the reason why young animals respond positively to their parents is that they recognize them as a source of food. Evidence was accumulating, however, to show that young animals and humans prefer individuals who offer comfort and affection over those who meet their physical needs. They show this preference by sticking as close as they can to parent figures, clinging or cuddling up to them (or, in the case of birds, following them). This behaviour is, not surprisingly, termed *attachment behaviour* (our daughter showed this clearly by physically grabbing the only accessible part of Joanna – her skirt). Bowlby postulated that it reflects a basic drive similar to, but independent of, hunger and thirst. He describes it thus in his work *A Secure Base*:

> Attachment behaviour is any form of behaviour that results in a person attaining or maintaining proximity to some other clearly identified individual, who is conceived as better able to cope with the world. It is most obvious when the person is frightened, fatigued or sick, and is assuaged by comforting and caregiving. At other times the behaviour is less in evidence. Nevertheless, for a person to know that an attachment figure is available and responsive gives him a strong and pervasive feeling of *security*, and so encourages him to value and continue the relationship. Whilst attachment behaviour is at its most obvious in early childhood, it can be observed throughout the life cycle, especially in emergencies. Since it is seen in virtually all human beings (though in varying patterns), it is regarded as an integral part of human nature, and one we share (to a varying extent) with members of other species. The biological function attributed to it is one of protection. To remain within easy access of a familiar individual known to be ready and willing to come to our aid in an emergency is clearly a good insurance policy – whatever our age (Bowlby 1988: 26–27, our emphasis).

Infants are apparently enabled to explore new environments by the presence of an attached adult. They will make forays away from the adult, but return rapidly if some change or threat is perceived. The adult is thus used as a secure base, and the infant gradually develops the courage to venture further afield, confident in the knowledge that the loved person is waiting for him or her. As adults we continue to encounter times when we need to hold someone's hand, perhaps in an intimidating social situation. Consider this description of the Lord Mayor's Reception at the Mansion House from George and Weedon Grossmith's Edwardian comedy *The Diary of a Nobody*:

> Crowds arrived, and I shall never forget the grand sight. My humble pen can never describe it. I was also a little annoyed with Carrie, who kept saying: 'Isn't it a pity we don't know anyone?' Once she quite lost her head. I saw someone who looked like Franching from Peckham, and was moving towards him when she seized me by the coat tails, and said quite loudly: 'Don't leave me', which caused an elderly gentleman, in a court suit and a chain round him, and two ladies to burst out laughing.

Thus extreme emotional distress can arise when temporary or permanent separation prevents one from attaching to the loved individual. The feelings that accompany separation in infants can only be guessed at. Anyone who observes such infants would use words such as *terror* or *panic* to describe their reactions. These reactions are probably triggered by the prospect of being *alone* or *abandoned*. Being completely alone is a universal and utterly devastating predicament. For mammals in particular, which originate from a physical attachment to the mother, the effects of such separation can indeed be poignant.

Bowlby was quick to point out the similarities between infant separation and adult bereavement. Death is, after all, the ultimate separation. Just as infants initially protest at being left, so newly bereaved adults find it hard to believe that they have lost a loved one. 'It can't be true' is a common reaction. Just as the infant calls for its mother, so the bereaved person searches for the deceased or sometimes mistakes other people for him or her. Dreams may be dominated by the loved one's return. There may be anger at being left behind. Later comes the despairing stage, when bitter grief is openly expressed. If the grief is not adequately resolved, a third stage of depression, analogous to infantile detachment, results. The concept of loss thus links separation to depression.

There is no doubt that disturbed attachment causes the infant distress at the time. Bowlby argues that its effects can persist into the future and are important factors in the development of the adult personality. He notes the high incidence of childhood separation experiences in the case of people who develop mental-health problems in adult life. However, he also suggests that disturbed *patterns* of attachment may be as damaging as complete severing of bonds. Extensive efforts have been made to verify Bowlby's theory empirically. The available evidence largely supports it. (However, it would be extremely difficult to verify it conclusively and to tease out all the possible causal agents at work in the parent–child relationship.)

According to this theory, while babies are all born with inherited temperamental differences, it is possible to identify certain patterns of parent and infant interaction predictive of later childhood behaviour. The optimal parental relationship is defined as *warm*, *continuous* and *intimate*. It need not be limited to the child's biological mother. Within such a relationship the child learns to value himself or herself. They internalize the belief that 'Because I am loved, because they are always there, because they accept me, I must be worth something.' Eventually the secure base provided by others (parents and peers) can be carried around as part of the person's psychological baggage. This is self-esteem.

Where the parental relationship is distorted by threats of abandonment or withdrawal of affection if certain demands are not met, then a pattern of dependent, clinging behaviour or cold, aloof withdrawal may occur. Where actual separation occurs, an internalization process along the following lines results: 'They left me, so I must be no good.' Where active abuse occurs, it is common for children to state, 'They hurt me. It must have been my fault.' The psychological baggage carried away from such relationships is a fragile or low self-esteem.

Bowlby's account can therefore be interpreted in this way: *self-esteem is one way in which people experience degrees of security or separation.*

Attachment behaviour seems to be universal to all humans regardless of culture. It also extends to the higher forms of animal life. It is therefore much more phylogenetically basic and universal than self-esteem, which, as was noted earlier, is limited to certain humans in certain social and historical contexts. We might speculate that the associations between self-esteem and personality function or mental health reflect a third factor, which causes them both. This third factor may be separation.

Where a secure, stable attachment has formed, we can begin to let go. The feeling of being at rest with the other is transformed into feelings of security about ourselves. If this does not occur, then the experience of separation anxiety, rejection or abandonment is potentially or actually all around us. We may try to distance ourselves from it by developing dependent relationships, over-investment in (*worship* of) career achievements or possessions, avoiding any threatening situations, or being preoccupied with ourselves: 'If I look in the mirror enough, I don't have to face the fact that I am alone.' These strategies reflect fragile, over-defended or just very low self-esteem.

Before closing this discussion, it is important to prevent a possible misunderstanding of Bowlby's account of optimal parenting. It is not necessary for the parental–child relationship to be *perfect*; it need only be *adequate*. This resonates with his psychotherapist colleague Donald Winnicott's account of 'good enough' mothering. It would be potentially damaging to suggest that unless parents behave in an optimal way towards their children *at all times*, they are laying the foundations of psychological disorder in later life. We should not fall into the trap of blaming our own parents for all our problems; nor should we castigate ourselves for our human limitations in not being perfect parents.

Let us now return to the four domains or areas from which self-esteem is drawn, described earlier in chapter 1. All four of these relate to attachment and separation:

Pedigree is obviously related to parental and family bonds.

The *love of another* is attachment by another name.

The *performance of roles* is one way the love of another can be earned or maintained, leading to attachment and the avoidance of separation.

Eternal significance is clearly a way in which death, the final separation, can be repudiated. By passing something of oneself on to people left behind, the impression of permanent attachment can be created.

Attachment theory is strongly biological and evolutionary in nature. The survival value of attachment behaviour is beyond dispute. But for the Christian, it is of deep interest and potential richness. In that the creation mirrors its Creator, however imperfectly, we can expect human relationships to point to aspects of our relation to God. The most obvious areas to be explored here are the images Scripture presents of God as our Father (and, to a lesser extent, as Mother). For example, the creation story tells us that, when God created Adam, the first thing he said was, 'It is not good for the man to be alone' (Gen. 2:18). (Interestingly, the first thing about creation that is not good relates to Adam's solitude.)

The biblical account tells us that, having grown from an ideally warm, continuous and intimate parental relationship, the adult is able to enter into another such relationship through attachment in marriage. The sexual act itself constitutes a physical attachment. 'For this reason a man will leave his father and mother and be united to his wife, and they will become one flesh' (Gen. 2:24). The marriage service draws our attention to the important role of the spouse as a comfort in time of trouble and an unconditionally secure base to whom one can return.

Nurturing aspects of the psychotherapeutic relationship

Chapter 1 briefly introduced the psychotherapeutic approach of Carl Rogers. This is of some interest if viewed in the context of attachment theory. In his book *On Becoming a Person*, Rogers identifies one basic problem affecting all people who come for psychological help. They are asking, 'Who am I, *really*? How can I get in touch with this real self underlying all my surface behaviour? How can I become myself?'

Rogerian client-centred therapy creates an environment in which the therapist encourages clients to 'discover themselves', without specifically directing them concerning the nature of that discovery. In other words, a *non-directive* approach is adopted, which deliberately avoids prescribing what the 'real self' is or ought to be like, in order that the client may establish this for himself or herself. This contrasts with the more directive approach of the cognitive behaviour therapist described earlier in this chapter.

The Rogerian therapist aims to assist the client to achieve a *knowledge* of this real self, and ultimately a *liking* of this real self. Where this process is taking place successfully, it is claimed that dramatic changes can be observed in the client:

> The individual becomes more integrated, more effective ... He changes his perception of himself, becoming more realistic in his views of the self. He becomes more like the person he wishes to be. He values himself more highly ... He becomes more accepting in his attitudes towards others, seeing others as more similar to himself (Rogers 1961: 36).

The context in which this journey of self-discovery and self-acceptance takes place is highly significant. The therapeutic *relationship* is absolutely vital. The effective therapist is characterized by *warmth, accurate empathy, genuineness* and *unconditional positive regard* for the client. In other words, the therapist must

- attempt to feel with and for the client
- show affection
- be open and honest
- be uncritical and accepting

These therapist characteristics have been demonstrated empirically to be associated with good outcome. The reader may recognize that such characteristics are almost identical to the warmth, continuity and intimacy that describe a good parental relationship. Indeed, Rogers argues that in therapy the client is enabled to admit first the positive feeling of the therapist towards him or her, and then, often after some difficulty and resistance, that 'I am worthy of being liked.' Thus the therapeutic relationship functions as an optimal parental relationship. 'I can permit someone to care about me and can fully accept that caring within myself. This permits me to recognize that I care, and care deeply, for and about others' (Rogers 1961: 86).

The link between the Rogerian account of self-acceptance and the present authors' explanation of self-esteem in terms of separation and security is exciting. However, it is not without substantial problems. The Rogerian approach involves laying aside moralism (that is, keeping a set of rules, such as 'shoulds' and 'oughts'). Ideas of 'duty' or 'obligation' are seen as inhibiting self-discovery. The client deliberately and systematically discounts the opinions of others in order to become his or her own judge. '1 did it my way' (Frank Sinatra) sums up this attitude. The ultimate measure of good personal adjustment is held to be autonomy. Autonomy and independence can even be seen as reasons to esteem the self. The client is enabled and encouraged to take responsibility to direct his or her own life. Most important of all, this humanistic theory asserts that 'the innermost core of man's nature is ... positive ... forward-looking, rational and realistic'. In other words, it is assumed that people are good and have an inherent capacity for self-improvement.

At this point the Christian comes into conflict with the secular accounts of human behaviour reviewed so far. These accounts throw valuable light upon the ways in which human psychological pain may be understood and, more importantly, relieved. In some respects their insights touch on the Christian understanding as set out in the Bible. But, while some theories might accommodate the existence of God with little trouble, others blame belief in God (and its associated guilt and fear) for psychopathology and human suffering, and none acknowledges the reality of sin. In the next chapter, we shall begin to examine this conflict in more detail.

4

Self-esteem: towards a Christian approach

It is natural that Christians should share the secular interest in self-esteem. This is not simply a response to the prevailing worldview; the gospel itself addresses a series of fundamental issues which are directly relevant to the concept of self-esteem. Rightly understood, the gospel first leads to a concern with self-esteem, and then shapes our understanding of this concept in a responsible and distinctively Christian way.

This distinctively Christian approach to self-esteem will lead to affirmation of some aspects of secular approaches and to radical criticism of others. Christians should neither reject nor affirm secular understandings of this issue uncritically. For example, nothing in this book should be taken to imply that secular therapeutic techniques are totally worthless. The genuine insights they contain, although limited, may be seen as resting on common grace (that is, in God's making himself known partially through the natural world and human values, as argued by Paul in Romans 1 – 2, and Acts 17). In addition, many ideas in western secular culture have been influenced unconsciously by Christian ideas and values. Some ideas that apparently arise within secular contexts actually have their origins in the Judeo-Christian tradition.

It is also possible to acknowledge the strengths of a particular psychological treatment without necessarily accepting all the ramifications of its underlying psychological and philosophical theory. The connection between technique and theory is much looser than is sometimes assumed. If a particular treatment (medical or psychological) is shown to be effective, this does not, on its own, validate the theory on which it is based. There may always be other explanations for the success of the treatment. For example, traditional herbal remedies were once thought to affect 'humours' (any of the four body fluids formerly considered responsible for human health) – an idea no longer taken seriously. Nevertheless, these remedies often worked.

For this reason, Christians should not be deterred from seeking help from or engaging with mainstream psychological approaches. Some of these approaches (for example, cognitive behaviour therapy) appear to work well in some respects. A technique which proves helpful may rest in part on a flawed understanding of human nature. Nevertheless, Christians may still benefit from it at a practical level, while remaining critical about some of the spiritual assumptions on which it is based.

This criticism needs to be applied in four major areas of tension between the Christian gospel and secular understandings of self-esteem:

- the reality of sin
- Christ's command that we should lose ourselves
- the Christian emphasis on moral absolutes
- the doctrine of salvation through divine grace, rather than human achievements

The reality of sin

Lord, do you hear me?
I'm suffering dreadfully. Locked in myself
Prisoner of myself
I hear nothing but my voice, I see nothing but myself
And behind me there is nothing but suffering. Lord, do you hear me?

Deliver me from my body; it is nothing but hunger, with its thousands of tentacles outstretched to appease its insatiable appetite.

Lord, do you hear me?

Deliver me from my heart; when I think that it's overflowing with love, I realize angrily that it is again myself that I love through the loved one. Lord, do you hear me?

Deliver me from my mind; it is full of itself, of its ideas, its opinions; it cannot carry on a dialogue, as no words reach it but its own.

Alone, I am bored, I am weary,

I hate myself,

I am disgusted with myself.

For ages I have been turning round inside myself like a sick man in his feverish bed.

Everything seems dark, ugly, horrid.

It's because I can only look through myself:

I feel ready to hate men and the whole world.

It's because I'm disappointed that I cannot love them. I would like to get away,

Walk, run, to another land.

I know that joy exists, I have seen it on singing faces. I know that light exists, I have seen it in radiant eyes.

But, Lord, I cannot get away, for I love my prison and I hate it,

For my prison is myself:

And I love myself, Lord.

I both love and loathe myself:

Lord, I can no longer find my own door. I grope around blindly,

I knock against my own walls, my own boundaries. I hurt myself, I am in pain

I am in too much pain, and no one knows it, for no one has come in.

I am alone, all alone.

Lord, Lord, do you hear me? Lord, show me my door:

Take me by the hand. Open the door,

Show me the way,

The path leading to joy, to light.

… But …

But, Lord, do you hear me?

Son, I have heard you. I am sorry for you.
I have long been watching your closed shutters; open them, my light
will come in.
I have long been standing at your locked door; open it, you will find
me on the threshold.
I am waiting for you, the others are waiting for you,
But you must open,
You must come out.
Why choose to be a prisoner of yourself? You are free.
It is not I who locked the door, It is not I who can open it.
... For it is you, from the inside, who persist in keeping it solidly
barred.

(Michel Quoist, 'Lord, do you hear me?')

Sin is the human longing to be like God, and a refusal to acknowledge our human limitations (Gen. 3). It can be seen as an act of rebellion and disobedience, in which humanity refused to accept the fact of its creatureliness, and tried to act as if it were God himself. The idea of sin is deeply counter-cultural within western society. Yet the biblical view is that sin is so deeply ingrained into the human personality that it cannot be ignored or marginalized. It must be acknowledged and addressed: 'If we claim to be without sin, we deceive ourselves and the truth is not in us' (1 John 1:8).

Sin has both objective and subjective aspects. It causes our relationship with God to be compromised and distorted, just as it causes our perceptions of God and ourselves to be seriously skewed. We *feel* alienated from God because we *are* alienated from God. We *feel* ourselves to be guilty in God's sight because we *are* guilty in his sight. To recognize that we are sinful is to see ourselves from God's perspective, as people who need forgiveness and redemption, and whose judgments concerning themselves, their situation and their identity are distorted.

This idea is found throughout the Bible and throughout the great Christian tradition of engaging with the biblical material. Sin is a multifaceted reality, impacting primarily upon our relationship with God, and as a consequence upon our perception of ourselves and our relationship with God. Sin is about wanting to go our own way, to do our own thing, to make our own judgments (Gen. 3).

It is therefore essential to challenge this human-centred perspective, by seeing things from God's viewpoint. Ideas of self-worth that are based upon an uncritical affirmation of human nature and values are incompatible with the Christian demand that our understanding of our nature, identity and destiny be grounded in God. Sin is a problem for us because it is a problem for God. The difficulty cannot be resolved by denying sin, or by treating it simply as a lack of self-fulfilment. It is something that needs forgiveness, healing and restoration from God's side. We cannot initiate this process of forgiveness and renewal; it is something that God alone can do. Part of the sheer wonder of the Christian gospel is its declaration that God has indeed done this, and that the cross of Christ is the means by which this amazing divine engagement with sin takes place.

As we have stressed, sin affects our relation with God, alienating us from his presence and power. As a result of our alienation from God, sin has a serious impact upon human thought and behaviour. Those looking for indications of sin from human experience need not look very far for confirmation. Nazism and Stalinism, and more recently genocidal events in Africa and parts of Europe, are abiding testimonies to the willingness of one group of human beings totally to eliminate another, convinced of their inferiority. Educated human beings have done serious damage to this planet, usually in pursuit of selfish material gains. Wars, exploitation and exclusion of groups defined by race or gender persist in the modern world, despite alleged advances in human civilization and technology.

The behaviour of societies, however, reflects the nature of their individual members. A sinful society is made up of sinful individuals. As Richard Dawkins points out in his significantly titled book *The Selfish Gene*, which explores aspects of the theory of evolution, there is a sense in which people are disposed to look out only for themselves. People act out of self-interest or extended self-interest. To give an obvious example, Dawkins argues that people are prepared to act for their children, not so much out of pure altruism, but in an evolutionarily determined manner, in order to save their own genes and ensure their survival in the gene pool of future generations.

Yet, as the prayer quoted above expresses, people are often deeply uncomfortable with this very situation. They aspire to a way of being that frees them from such self-interest. Themes of guilt and self-criticism often emerge as part of this personal struggle.

Secular therapies too often ignore this or contradict it by repudiating any sense of personal guilt. In particular, both cognitive therapy and Rogerian therapy seem to minimize the negative personal or individual moral dimensions of the human situation, in rejecting ideas such as blame or guilt, and the vital, related notion of repentance. Thus cognitive therapy assumes that rational thinking is integral to mental health. Yet the English theologian and archbishop William Temple (1881–1944) dismissed such an unwarranted assumption about human nature. Educate people, he argued, and all you do is raise them up and broaden their horizons. But they remain centred on themselves. They may see further; their thoughts, however, remain obstinately centred on their own selfish needs and appetites. Rationality is employed to pursue their own ends. Being rational therefore does not stop people from being immoral. Often it simply allows them to pursue their own agendas and achieve their own goals more effectively, regardless of the effect on others. One of the most tragic aspects of the sinful human situation is that human rationality can be directed towards the pursuit of power and material goods just as well as to the alleviation of the world's problems.

It must be made clear that rationality is important, and that it plays an important role in human well-being. But irrationality is only a tiny fraction of the sinful predicament in which human beings find themselves. Totally rational people are capable of acting in immoral and selfish ways.

The therapeutic approach developed by Carl Rogers works on the basis of the related assumption that if people accept themselves, they will be psychologically healthy human beings. But what if there really is something wrong with human nature? What if we are being asked to accept something that is inherently unacceptable? Can we seriously believe that a Nazi extermination-camp commandant could really accept himself, in the light of all that he had done, seen and ordered? The Christian view is that *repentance*, arising from a genuine sense of sorrow and contrition, must be an integral element of authentic self-acceptance.

Yet repentance plays an insignificant part in secular approaches to counselling and psychology. It is often regarded as an unhelpful or unacceptable notion. This view thus denies to individuals the possibility of coping fully with their past, knowing that it has been set behind them and forgiven.

In turning to deal with the biblical view of human nature, we encounter a refreshing and direct realism. Humanity is sinful. Human beings are separated from God on account of sin: 'your iniquities have separated you from your God; your sins have hidden his face from you' (Is. 59:2).

We can explore three biblical images that develop this theme of separation from God.

First, *alienation from God*. Paul reminds his readers that they were once 'separate from Christ, excluded from citizenship in Israel and foreigners to the covenants of the promise, without hope and without God in the world' (Eph. 2:12). Sin is like being at war with God (Eph. 2:14–16). Yet that hostility can be overcome. Christ is our peace, in that he has broken down the hostility between ourselves and God. He has made it possible for us to be reconciled to God, so that our alienation is abolished (2 Cor. 5:19). Through Christ, we have been restored to fellowship with God.

Secondly, *expulsion from paradise*. On account of sin, Adam and Eve were expelled from Eden (Gen. 3:24). There could be no return to Eden; the way was blocked by the cherubim and flaming sword. These are powerful images of the separation between God and humanity. Sin is a barrier between ourselves and paradise, and the God who created us to dwell there. We have become 'foreigners and aliens' (Eph. 2:19), wandering the face of the earth in lonely isolation. Yet, through faith, we enter into a community – the people of God. Through Christ we are now 'fellow-citizens with God's people and members of God's household' (Eph. 2:19). Notice again how salvation is understood as being restored to fellowship with God. The barriers of separation have been overcome and removed. Heaven can thus be seen as our final and permanent restoration to the presence of God.

An important related idea is that of *rejection*. The expulsion of

Adam and Eve from Eden is an aspect of their rejection by God. On account of their sin, they are denied access to the presence of God and to the blessings he had intended for them. Sin excludes us from the fellowship of God. This does not arise on account of some human inability to find God. It is a result of disobedience, a decision to reject God. In order for the situation to be changed and for fellowship to be restored, God must be able to accept those whom he has rejected. Once more, the importance of the theme of *reconciliation* will be obvious. Through the saving death of Christ on the cross, God accepts those who were once unacceptable, and brings close those who were far away.

Thirdly, *going our own way*. 'We all, like sheep, have gone astray, each of us has turned to his own way' (Is. 53:6). Choosing to go our own way inevitably means departing both from God's way and from God himself. Our desire for autonomy leads us to take paths of our own choosing which lead away from the God who created us. Perhaps one of Jesus' most memorable parables concerns a son who decides to go his own way (Luke 15:11–24). That act of 'going his own way' meant that the son decided to leave his father's presence and ignore his will and purposes. Eventually, the son deeply regretted his action and longed to be restored to his father's presence. The story of the son's restoration to fellowship with his father is one of the most moving and powerful narratives in Scripture. The importance in this context will be clear: going our own way means going away from God, and becoming separated from him.

Biblical images of sin such as these lead us to an understanding that the core consequences of sin are separation from God at the *physical, personal* and *moral* level. At the *physical level*, we are cut off from God on account of death, which is an integral aspect of sin. Through faith, we are assured of eternal life, in which we shall never again experience separation from God. 'For the wages of sin is death, but the gift of God is eternal life in Christ Jesus our Lord' (Rom. 6:23). At the *personal level*, our relationship of love and trust with God has been spoiled.

At the *moral level*, we are no longer in good standing with God. This is expressed in the Bible in terms of our unrighteousness in the light of God's holiness and justice: 'the LORD Almighty will be exalted by his justice, and the holy God will show himself holy by his righteousness'(Is. 5:16). The importance of the concept of righteousness, and its relationship to self-esteem, will be discussed in the next chapter.

Obviously, a real tension exists between the inherent optimism of many secular psychotherapies and what the American writer Reinhold Niebuhr (1892–1971) described as 'Christian realism'. This realism recognizes the reality and seriousness of human sin in the face of the delusions of those who wish to overlook it. In this connection, it is of interest to note that there is evidence to suggest that depressed people may actually have a *more* realistic grasp of their situation than their 'normal' counterparts, whose mental health is somehow protected by an optimistic bias.

A responsible Christian approach to self-esteem must steep itself in the harsh fact of sin. Secular therapies may find the idea of sin to be 'unhelpful'; but if it is *true*, it cannot be ignored in any responsible and reliable evaluation of the human situation.

Christ's command that we should lose ourselves

A second area of tension is indicated by Christ's emphasis upon self-denial. This major New Testament theme plays a central role in all Christian thinking on holiness, whether catholic or evangelical. It is of such significance that it must be given considerable weight in any discussion of self-esteem. 'Whoever tries to keep his life will lose it, and whoever loses his life will preserve it' (Luke 17:33). The Bible asks us to lose our lives in order to gain them. We are called to servanthood, humility and obedience, and to a will that is not our own. We are to give up attempts to control our own destiny, and trust ourselves to God's will for us (Luke 22:42). We are thus called away from the autonomy that is so greatly prized by Rogers and others.

Let us at this point consider the nature of the 'original sin' of Genesis 3. Underlying the famous story of the rebellion of Adam and Eve against God is the motif of self-sufficiency. If you eat of the fruit of this tree, you will be like God. You will be able to decide for yourself what is right and wrong. You can manage without God. A basic feature of fallen human nature is the craving for autonomy, the passionate pursuit of the cult of self-sufficiency. From their mother's knee upwards, many people are taught that any form of dependency is unhealthy and unwholesome. These attitudes are further reinforced by the pressures of modern western society with its emphasis upon individual success.

Now it must be clear that the Christian idea of losing oneself has nothing to do with the Buddhist idea of dissolving into an impersonal mass. At its heart, the gospel is concerned with two competing ideas of freedom and autonomy. We could describe them as follows.

First, the view that *we are masters of our own souls*. Nothing compromises our freedom except obstacles that we needlessly place in the way of that autonomy. Historically, this approach is usually described as Pelagian, after the fourth-century writer Pelagius, who emphasized the total freedom and responsibility of humans.

Secondly, the view that *our natural freedom is a spurious autonomy*. It is compromised by sin, which places severe, yet largely unrecognized, limitations upon our freedom. We labour under the delusion that we are free, and yet we are really in bondage. This outlook is associated with Augustine of Hippo, Pelagius' most acute and discerning critic.

Augustine comes much closer than Pelagius to Christ's demand that we lose ourselves in order to find ourselves. We must surrender our natural fallen freedom, a freedom tainted and compromised by sin even if we do not realize it. As Augustine stressed, this 'freedom' is in reality only a freedom to serve sin and remain trapped in our sinful situation. And in its place, we are to receive – as a gift – a real freedom, which comes only from being liberated from the bondage of sin. Christian writers have always recognized the central paradox of Christian obedience: it is only by serving God that we have perfect freedom. It is only by becoming God's slaves that we become free men and women.

This theme occurs throughout Scripture. To give a helpful example: we are asked to give up our spurious idea of 'life' as mere biological existence that must end in physical death. And having done this, we can receive a new *life – eternal life* – which alone is 'life ... in all its fullness' (John 10:10, Revised English Bible). We lose the shadow in order to gain the reality. We abandon what is temporary and transient in order to gain what is permanent and eternal.

Scripture playfully compares our natural and fallen freedom with that of a flock of sheep. Time and time again, sinners are compared to sheep, who are utterly helpless unless they are fortunate enough to be tended by a caring shepherd (Ps. 23; Luke 15:3–7; John 10:1–15). Sheep possess autonomy. Yet in exercising that freedom, all they manage to do is get lost and fall into danger. Indeed, Scripture uses the image of sheep without a shepherd to describe people who are totally lost and bewildered (Zech. 10:2; Mark 6:34). Freedom is no guarantee of being able to cope with life. We need to be guided and assisted and liberated from the tyranny of sin.

It is perhaps at this point that the full wonder of the Christian doctrine of redemption becomes apparent. The Shepherd gives up his life in order that his sheep may live. Christ dies in order that we who merely exist may have life in all its fullness. Christ willingly sets his own life to one side so that we can live. As St Paul points out, one of the greatest paradoxes of faith is that only the person who has died is freed from sin (Rom. 6:7). Yet in dying to sin – that is, in dying to our natural state of sin, mortality and transience – we are born again to eternal life. We must therefore consider ourselves as 'dead to sin but alive to God in Christ Jesus' (Rom. 6:11).

Secular approaches assume that we do not need to question the way we are. We need not seek anything beyond the realm of this world. And, for the Christian, this inevitably means that those who rely upon secular therapies will remain captive to sin. Paradoxically, such approaches can be allies of sin, in that they prevent us from escaping from its clutches, asserting that there is no bondage in the first place. Once more, the importance of the Christian insistence upon the reality of sin will become clear. No Christian can rest content with this shallow assessment of the human predicament.

The Christian emphasis upon absolute moral standards

Cognitive behaviour therapy and Rogerian approaches deny the existence and helpfulness of absolute moral standards. These approaches see the aim for high absolute moral standards as pathological; instead, they argue, we should lower our standards to be 'realistic' and 'attainable'. There is an assumption that perfection is unattainable. Thus, striving for perfection can only bring disappoinment and frustration, whereas the actual achievement of more attainable goals gives a sense of success, a beneficial experience that enhances self-esteem.

Yet Christ adopts a rather different approach. In Matthew's account of the Sermon on the Mount, Jesus describes himself as the ultimate fulfilment of the Old Testament law (itself underpinned by the moral absolutes enshrined in the Ten Commandments). 'Be perfect, therefore, as your heavenly Father is perfect' (Matt. 5:48). This absolute demand cannot be ignored. For Christians, absolute moral standards cannot be regarded as arbitrary pragmatic human rules of thumb, but only as something established by God. They reflect something real about the nature of God and the world he created. They are not mere human social conventions.

Underlying this tension between Christian and secular approaches is a real difference in worldviews. The secular therapist views success as something that enhances self-esteem; thus it is to be commended. The Christian sees failure as something of, if anything, more potential value, bringing home to us our weakness and frailty and encouraging us to rely more upon the grace of God, rather than upon our own resources and ability.

A paradigm for this transformation of failure experiences is the relationship between Jesus and Peter, vividly revealed in the Gospel narratives. Peter is a chronic mistake-maker. His impulsive and argumentative behaviour gets him into trouble on numerous occasions (see for instance Matt. 14:28–31; Mark 8:31–33; John 13:6–11; 18:10–11). His human weaknesses reach a climax in his denial of Jesus three times in the house of the high priest:

> Now Peter was sitting out in the courtyard, and a servant girl came to him. 'You also were with Jesus of Galilee,' she said.
>
> But he denied it before them all. 'I don't know what you're talking about,' he said.
>
> Then he went out to the gateway, where another girl saw

him and said to the people there, 'This fellow was with Jesus of Nazareth.'

He denied it again, with an oath: 'I don't know the man!'

After a little while, those standing there went up to Peter and said, 'Surely you are one of them, for your accent gives you away.'

Then he began to call down curses on himself and he swore to them, 'I don't know the man!'

Immediately a cock crowed. Then Peter remembered the word Jesus had spoken: 'Before the cock crows, you will disown me three times.' And he went outside and wept bitterly (Matt. 26:69–75).

Peter is overwhelmed with remorse. In John's account, after the resurrection, Jesus sensitively allows Peter to use this remorse to good effect, asking Peter to state his love for him three times. After what is essentially an act of repentance on Peter's part, Jesus does him the unparalleled honour of entrusting the church into his hands:

... Jesus said to Simon Peter, 'Simon son of John, do you truly love me more than these?'

'Yes, Lord,' he said, 'you know that I love you.'

Jesus said, 'Feed my lambs.'

Again Jesus said, 'Simon son of John, do you truly love me?'

He answered, 'Yes, Lord, you know that I love you.'

Jesus said, 'Take care of my sheep.'

The third time he said to him, 'Simon son of John, do you love me?'

Peter was hurt because Jesus asked him the third time, 'Do you love me?' He said, 'Lord, you know all things; you know that I love you.'

Jesus said, 'Feed my sheep' (John 21:15–17).

The Christian is thus enabled to value and learn from failure. The secular therapist has some difficulty with failure and adopts the somewhat defeatist attitude of lowering standards in order that everyone may succeed. But at the heart of the gospel lies the insight that God's standards are not some trivial human invention that can be discarded at will. The secular therapist is, in effect, obliged to say something like, 'If at first you don't succeed, change the rules!' The Christian can say with confidence that we may learn more about ourselves and about God by keeping the rules just the way they are.

In the eyes of the world, failure is linked with rejection. To fail at a task or in a role is likely to mean rejection by important others. The Christian perspective is radically different. The love of God was made known in an act of apparent failure – the death of Christ. What the world counts as failure is transfigured by God's reversal of the world's standards. 'But God chose the foolish things of the world to shame the wise; God chose the weak things of the world to shame the strong. He chose the lowly things of this world and the despised things – and the things that are not – to nullify the things that are, so that no-one may boast before him' (1 Cor. 1:27–29). In short, God chose what the world rejected and despised as failure (1 Pet. 2:6–7).

We shall explore some of the issues posed by the persistence of sin in believers in the following chapter. Our attention now turns briefly to the doctrine of grace.

Salvation by divine grace, not by human achievements

The Reformation rediscovered that we cannot base our salvation, acceptability to ourselves or God, on our works or achievements. The attitude of Jesus to such things as wealth, status, achievements, the love of others and pedigree make this clear.

Wealth. 'It is easier for a camel to go through the eye of a needle than for a rich man to enter the kingdom of God' (Matt. 19:24). Jesus discounts the value of riches, even seeing them as an impediment to entering the kingdom of God. Money does not influence his estimation of people.

Reputation. 'Woe to you when all men speak well of you' (Luke 6:26). Jesus declares that a person's reputation among his or her peers does not affect God's regard for the person.

Possessions. '"You fool! This very night your life will be demanded from you. Then who will get what you have prepared for yourself?" This is how it will be with anyone who stores up things for himself but is not rich toward God' (Luke 12:20–21). The accumulation of possessions may enhance someone's prestige in the world – but it cuts no ice with God.

Wisdom. 'Where is the wise man? Where is the scholar? Where is the philosopher of this age? Has not God made foolish the wisdom of the world?' (1 Cor. 1:20). The wisdom that gives us status in the eyes of the world has little value in the sight of God.

In the cognitive behavioural model (and other related psychotherapeutic approaches), external achievements are seen as enhancing self-esteem. While such approaches recognize that simply trying to buy love or approval through achievement is misguided, if not impossible, perceived external success remains a vital component of self-esteem for them. There is no doubt that adequate role assumption *does* relate to acceptance by other people, precisely because it gives us a place in the social network.

Jesus' radical approach undercuts this reliance on achievement and is in fact echoed in some secular psychotherapeutic approaches (e.g. the Jungian), which regard over-investment in achievement as unhealthy. However, while such therapies advocate laying aside spurious sources of self-esteem, they do not say what should be put in their place. The gospel remedies this deficiency, as we shall see. It does not merely mount a sustained critique of the role of human achievement in relation to self-esteem; it offers a new basis for that self-esteem.

The idea of 'justification by works' is important in this respect. Just as some Jews appear to have thought that one could find acceptance with God by rigorously observing the law of Moses, so many contemporary therapeutic approaches assume that self-acceptance can rest upon success and achievement. The quest for acceptability, to oneself or in the sight of others, often proceeds on the belief that such acceptance is contingent, at least in part, upon adequate role behaviour – such as being a good mother, a successful athlete, a creative artist, or someone others will look up to. This is a more subtle form of justification by works than keeping a set of rules or passing a set of tests. Yet the entire thrust of the Christian doctrine of grace is that acceptance – both in our own eyes and in God's – cannot depend upon anything we do.

What, then, are we to make of the findings reviewed earlier in this book? It seems that much human misery centres around failure to value ourselves and finds its extreme in suicide and self-destructive behaviour. Christians are not exempt from this experience. Some may even feed their own negative self-esteem by an excessive appeal to scriptural passages that emphasize sin, guilt and alienation. Others may find that negative self-esteem is reinforced by a church culture that majors on criticism and exhortation, rather than on affirmation, from the pulpit.

As we have seen, Christianity places strong emphasis upon the reality of sin, the desirability of self-loss and dependence, the existence of absolute moral standards, the inability of people to meet these standards through their own efforts, and the need for repentance. This emphasis might be taken to mean that Christianity undervalues people or perpetuates emotional pain, inner conflict and guilt – perhaps even contributing to the genesis of mental illness. Yet this is not the case.

We have yet to consider the Christian *response* to such matters as sin and guilt – the person of Jesus Christ and his redeeming work upon the cross. Through the death and resurrection of Jesus Christ, God bridges the seemingly absolute gap between the reality of human sin, hopelessness and helplessness, and his own absolute moral purity and holiness. He purges our guilt, which we could never purge ourselves. Through the cross, God affirms us when we are undeserving of affirmation. He judges us worthy when we honestly and accurately see ourselves as unworthy. He meets our basic need for attachment despite the fact that we are separated from him.

This naturally brings us to a discussion of the doctrine of grace – the assertion that God has met us and fulfilled us in Christ. Our separation from God, personal, moral and physical, has been abolished through the work of Christ on the cross, which we accept and make our own through faith. We now consider how the cross of Christ provides the objective basis for Christian self-esteem.

5

The cross:
the objective basis of
self-esteem

One of the major themes resounding throughout the Christian
discussion of redemption is that of God's justice and righteousness.
God does not redeem us in some arbitrary and haphazard manner,
but in a way that both accords with and declares his righteousness.
It is therefore natural that the imagery and language of the
lawcourt should find its way into Christian discourse about the
meaning of the cross.

The cross and sin

Perhaps one of the most important aspects of this way of
approaching the cross relates to sin. Sin can be understood in
moral, legal or penal terms. It is an offence against God. Sin is not
a trivial offence, like being rude to someone. Sin violates the moral
order of the creation established by God himself at the foundation
of the world. Sin tears the moral fabric of the creation, a structure
that reflects God's nature.

So how can God forgive human sin without himself violating
that moral order? Why can't God just forgive sin and have done
with it? Why not just declare that all sin, past, present and future,
is cancelled and forgiven? Because this would be to treat sin in the

most shockingly shallow manner. It would deny its seriousness. It would fail to safeguard the creation against corruption and contamination. It would make a mockery of justice, pretending that sin is just some private matter, of no public relevance.

It is here that the cross becomes of central importance. It condemns sin, showing up its full seriousness. Sin, which might seem a trivial issue, leads to the state of affairs where God himself ends up being crucified. So perverted and confused has the moral ordering of the creation become on account of human sin that the creation ends up attempting to destroy its Creator. Something radical has to be done to restore the harmony of the world, to cancel its guilt in order that it may start again, and to break the power of disruptive forces within.

Yet so deeply is the creation, and supremely human nature, enmeshed in sin that it cannot get itself out of its guilt-ridden situation. People are trapped, wallowing around in a mud pit of introspective self-centredness. So great is our accumulation of sin, guilt and inherited punishment that we cannot hope to break free. Like a bad debt, it keeps getting bigger, with no hope of wiping it out and starting all over again. A web of guilt has been spun from which there is no escape. Only action from outside can enable us to break free from this self-imposed prison.

The cross marks a turning-point in this situation. It ends our enmity with God. God's relation to us changes – and thus enables our relationship with him to change. Christ broke down the barrier sin posed to our friendship with God. The temple curtain at Jerusalem symbolized for many the inability of ordinary people to enter into God's presence – hence their separation from God. This curtain was torn at the time of Christ's death. The tearing itself is a powerful symbol of the way the death of Christ broke down the barrier of sin that prevented us from coming into God's presence. The way has been opened for us to return to God. Separation from God can become reconciliation to God, and thus attachment to God.

In Jesus Christ, God has taken upon himself the burden of human guilt. Christ is the one who bore the weight of human sin upon his lonely and tired shoulders at Calvary (Is. 53:10–12; 1 Pet. 2:24). 'God made him who had no sin to be sin for us, so that in

him we might become the righteousness of God' (2 Cor. 5:21).
Christ was content to be reckoned among sinners in order to
redeem sinners (Is. 53:12). 'He himself bore our sins in his body
on the tree, so that we might die to sins and live for righteousness;
by his wounds you have been healed' (1 Pet. 2:24). The cross
brings home both the seriousness of sin and the power and purpose
of God to engage with it, eventually to destroy it. In the cross we
see *real* forgiveness of *real* sins – our sins. The initiative was from
God; the response must be from us. God moved so that we can
move. God loved us in order that we might love him.

Although holy and guiltless in himself, Jesus was thus cut off
from God by the moral weight of human sin. He chose to become
sin in order that we might become righteous in the sight of God.
The dying Christ took sin, which causes a moral separation
between ourselves and God, upon himself, thus removing this
barrier between God and us. No obstacle now prevents our being
attached to God.

But Jesus also became physically separated from God. He felt
the full weight of this separation, as we see clearly in the dreadful
cry of dereliction: 'My God, my God, why have you forsaken me?'
(Mark 15:34). Jesus here shared our separation from God, sensing
the pain and loneliness of his absence. Through the cross of Christ,
this vital aspect of separation from God is dealt with. Christ
became separated from God in order that we might become reattached to him through faith in what Christ achieved.

God thus did what only he could do. He took away both the
guilt and the power of human sin. He was under no obligation to
do so. But in his mercy and compassion, he chose to act in this
way. At no point is his righteousness compromised. Such is his love
for us that he takes upon himself the pain and suffering which, by
rights, should have been ours. As Paul once wrote, 'I live by faith
in the Son of God, who loved me and gave himself for me' (Gal.
2:20).

But how are we to understand the mystery of just how the cross
brings this about? There are three main ways of making sense of
what happened.

First, *representation*. Christ is here understood to be the
covenant representative of humanity. Through faith, we come to

stand within the covenant between God and humanity. All that Christ has won for us through the cross is available to us on account of the covenant. Just as God entered into a covenant with his people Israel, so he has entered into a covenant with his church. Christ, by his obedience upon the cross, represents his covenant people, winning benefits for them as their representative. By coming to faith, individuals share in all covenant benefits won by Christ through his cross and resurrection – including the full and free *forgiveness* of our sins.

Secondly, *participation*. Through faith, believers participate in the risen Christ. They are 'in Christ', to use Paul's famous phrase. They are caught up in him and share in his risen life. As a result of this, they share in all the benefits won by Christ through his obedience upon the cross. Participating in Christ thus entails the forgiveness of our sins and sharing in his righteousness.

Thirdly, *substitution*. Christ is here understood to be our substitute, the one who goes to the cross in our place. There is no limit to the extent to which Christ is prepared to identify with us. We ought to have been crucified on account of our sins. Christ is crucified in our place. God allows Christ to stand in our place, taking our guilt upon himself, so that his righteousness – won by obedience upon the cross – might become ours. Christ enters into our human situation, sharing its sorrows, its pain and its guilt. And all these are brought to the cross. They are nailed to that cross, along with the one who bears them for us. By his wounds we are healed.

The cross, then, establishes the objective basis of Christian self-esteem. It is here that God has established his relationship with us. Sin has been dealt with. Where secular psychological theories close their eyes to the reality, the seriousness and the power of sin, the gospel acknowledges them – but strongly affirms the reality, the seriousness and the power of the cross of Christ to defeat sin. We may rest assured that all that is necessary for self-esteem has been done – and done extremely well! – by God through Christ on the cross.

Despite this, some people still have difficulty with the idea that sinners can be acceptable in the sight of God. How, they ask, can God value us when we are still sinners? In view of the importance of this question, we shall answer it in full, looking at the relevance of the doctrine of justification by faith in some detail. This doctrine, of central importance to the writings of St Paul, deals with the question of how sinners can find acceptance in the sight of a righteous and holy God. Paul Tillich, a twentieth-century American writer, declared that the doctrine of justification by faith means 'accepting that you are accepted, despite being unacceptable'. We shall see how this is the case.

Images of wholeness: the New Testament on salvation

The New Testament uses a rich range of powerful images to express what God has done for us in Christ. Each of these images casts light on a different facet of the Christian understanding of the newness of life that comes about through faith. One of the central ideas of the New Testament is that a radical change in our status comes about when faith unites us to Christ. Each image explored here is charged with relevance for a properly Christian understanding of self-esteem.

Ransomed by Christ

As he neared the end of his life, Christ told his disciples that he had come 'to give his life as a ransom for many' (Mark 10:45). This is a powerful way of making sense of the meaning of the cross. It immediately conveys the idea of liberation – being set free from prison or bondage – just as Christians have been set free from bondage to sin and the fear of death and enter into the glorious liberty of the children of God.

But it implies more than that. It also points to the payment of a price so that we may go free. A ransom is a payment that secures someone's liberation. And the New Testament affirms that the price paid for our redemption is the death of the Son of God. The idea of a ransom price holds the key to some vital Christian insights into self-esteem.

Imagine that someone has been captured and held for ransom by a group of international kidnappers. The price set for her release is enormous. Initially, she believes that she can raise the funds.

However, she gradually realizes that she is too poor. A sense of despair and despondency sets in. She begins to face up to the fact that she may never be released, resigning herself to her fate.

Yet a group of friends has resolved to do something to help. Unknown to her, they join together to raise the substantial sum of money demanded for her release. To her amazement and joy, the ransom demand is paid. She is freed!

That story is simple, and yet it offers us invaluable insights into how our self-esteem can and should be grounded in the cross of Christ. The gospel tells us that we are held captive by a coalition of forces, such as sin and death. We are unable to break free from them. Like kidnappers, they hold us for ransom and we are unable to pay that ransom demand. As a result, we are in a hopeless situation. We are doomed to remain in bondage – unless someone else cares for us enough to work for our release.

Imagine the change in this woman's self-esteem. Initially, it sinks to rock bottom when she discovers that she cannot change her situation. In her own eyes, she is devoid of value. But then the situation changes radically. She discovers that she is valued by others. Her self-worth now rests on the attitude of others towards her – an attitude expressed in their determination to help and their willingness to raise the substantial sum of money involved.

The gospel declares that God is both determined to save us and prepared to pay the price salvation entails. Paul reminded his Corinthian readers that they had been bought at the price of the death of the Son of God (1 Cor. 6:20; 7:23). God values us so much that he gave his own Son that we might be free.

Reconciliation

A similar line of thought arises from another of Paul's central ideas: reconciliation. 'God was reconciling the world to himself in Christ' (2 Cor. 5:19). The image is that of a broken personal relationship, which needs to be healed. Reconciliation would replace a state of enmity with God by a state of friendship and trust. Christianity, to put it very simply, is about becoming a friend of God, with all that true friendship implies.

Earlier we noted how our self-esteem was partly determined by the social group with which we associate. Our peer group affects the way we view ourselves, just as it affects the way others regard us. To belong to the *right* club, the *right* crowd or the *right* set is seen by many as of central importance to one's personal image and social standing. Reconciliation allows Christians to speak of themselves as being friends with God, valuing themselves in consequence. The parable of the prodigal son (Luke 15:11–24), in which the son and father meet halfway, provides a marvellous example of the importance of reconciliation and hints at its implications for the reconciled son's self-esteem. It is only when he is reconciled that his father orders the fatted calf to be killed for a celebratory feast. Think of what that must have done for the wayward son's self-esteem!

But there is more to this image. Imagine a child waking up in the middle of the night, frightened of the dark. Anxiously, he calls for his mother. She comes to his bedside, holds him by the hand, and says, 'There, there. It's *all right*'. But what is all *right*? The really important thing here is that the child, who had felt separated from his mother, can now draw comfort from her presence. Things are 'all right' because she is there. She is by his side, and that enables him to cope with the dark and the unknown threats of the night. 'Right' here is not a moral concept; it is a rightness of presence. 'Things are right, now that I am here.'

Reconciliation is about our being restored to the comforting presence of God. It is about enabling us to face the unknown future in the presence of a known and loved God. The separation resulting from sin is ended; in its place, we are enabled to experience and delight in the presence and power of God. We shall explore further in the next chapter the idea of the parental care of God.

Salvation

The key term 'salvation' is used frequently in the New Testament (see Acts 13:26; Eph. 1:13; Heb. 1:14). The way the idea is used in the New Testament (where the verb is generally in the future tense) suggests that it should be thought of as a future event – something still to happen, although it may have begun to happen in the present. The basic idea is that of deliverance, preservation or rescue from a dangerous situation. The verb is used outside the New Testament to refer to being saved from death by the intervention of a rescuer, or to being cured of a deadly illness. It can also refer to being kept in good health. The Jewish historian Josephus used the word *salvation* to refer to the deliverance of the Israelites from Egyptian bondage.

The concept suggests two ideas. First, one may be *rescued or delivered from a dangerous situation* – just as the Israelites were delivered from their captivity in Egypt at the time of the exodus. So Christ is understood to deliver us from the fear of death and the power of sin. The name 'Jesus' means 'God saves' – and it is clear that the New Testament means 'saves from sin' (Matt. 1:21 is important here).

The second idea is that of *wholeness or health*. There is a very close relation between the ideas of salvation and wholeness. In many languages, the words for 'health' and 'salvation' are one and the same. Thus it is sometimes difficult to know whether a passage should be translated in terms of salvation or of wholeness. For example, should the Greek of Mark 5:34 be translated as 'Your faith has made you whole' or 'Your faith has saved you'? This close association of ideas was also found in the English language until the time of the Norman Conquest in 1066. The Old English word for 'salvation' (*hoel* – note the similarity to the modern English words *heal* and *health*) was replaced by the Latin form *salvation* at that time, with the result that the English-speaking world has lost this close association of both the words and the concepts. But in some other modern languages, this association remains. Let us explore its meaning.

When people who have been ill are healed, they are restored to their former state of health, of wholeness. The creation accounts (Gen. 1 – 2) make it clear that God created us in a state of wholeness, and this wholeness was lost through the fall (Gen. 3). Just as healing involves restoration to health, so salvation involves restoration to wholeness – restoration to the state in which we were first created by God. Paul draws attention to the relation between the first Adam and the second (Christ): through Adam we lost our integrity before God; through Christ that integrity can be regained and restored. In many respects the gospel is like a medicine – something that heals us even though we don't fully understand how it works.

It is helpful to notice the close link between sin and disease in the Gospels (as in Matt. 9:6). Jesus healed people and forgave their sins, and both activities are aspects of the restoration to wholeness which is God's gift to us in Christ.

This, then, outlines the basic meaning of salvation. But what bearing does it have on self-esteem? How does thinking about the meaning of salvation encourage us to value ourselves in a properly Christian manner?

Illness is a central biblical model for sin. Sin is like a disease, which God cures through the work of Christ on the cross. Most of us feel profoundly unworthy of the love of God on account of our selfishness and guilt. For many Christians, a proper Christian sense of self-worth is fatally compromised through sin. How can God value someone like me when I am a sinner? How can God really love someone as worthless as me, tainted and contaminated by my sin?

The Christian doctrine of salvation has some vitally important insights to offer here. First, it affirms that we really are sinners – but sinners in the process of being renewed and transformed. Augustine of Hippo, a noted early Christian writer, once likened the church to a hospital. It is a community of sick people, united by their willingness to acknowledge their sin and by their hope and trust in the skill of the physicians to whose care they are committed. The sin that is now so real and obvious an aspect of their lives will one day be fully removed. But God can love his people *now*. He can anticipate the final removal of our sin and love us now in the light of what we will be on that final day.

So Christian self-esteem should not be compromised by an awareness of sin. We Christians should not despise or hate ourselves on account of the continuing presence of sin in our lives. A sense of guilt is appropriate for the sins we commit while we are Christians. But those sins can be confessed and forgiven. After that, we need not feel guilty for being sinners. As we have emphasized, the gospel affirms that we are *forgiven sinners*. To retain a sense of guilt for being sinners is to overlook the vital fact of our forgiveness! We can also cripple our spiritual growth through failing to realize that the penalty of sin has been paid through the cross, so that we labour under the delusion that we are somehow being asked to pay that penalty ourselves. Our sin has been nailed to the cross of Christ, and it should remain there.

God makes a vital distinction between sin and the sinner, promising to deliver us from the penalty, power and presence of sin. That penalty has been paid through the cross of Christ. That power is being broken through the presence of the risen Christ in our lives.

And finally, on the last day, we shall be freed once and for all from the presence of sin. But in the meantime, we must learn to accept that we are like sick people, entrusted to the care of a loving and healing God, just as the good Samaritan entrusted his wounded friend to the care of the innkeeper (Luke 10:25–37). God knows that we are ill and has promised to heal us. And we must learn to value ourselves responsibly, by seeing beyond our sinful present to our redeemed future.

Justification by faith

To speak of 'justification by faith' is immediately to run into a serious difficulty. The phrase sounds strange to modern ears. 'Justification' is most commonly understood today as a defence of one's position in an argument or legal case, or as achieving a straight right-hand edge in a block of text by varying the space between words. So how can a term most familiar from the worlds of justice and word-processing have any real relevance for Christian self-esteem?

The English word *justification*, in its theological sense, is an attempt to denote the Old Testament idea of being 'right before God'. Through a complex tradition of translation and interpretation – from Hebrew to Greek, from Greek to Latin, and finally from Latin to English – *justification* has come to refer to the status of being righteous in the sight of God. To be justified is to be right with God. But this idea of 'being right with God' is relational rather than moral. It is primarily about the way in which we relate to God, not about any moral or ethical qualities we may possess. For the German Reformer Martin Luther (1483–1546), to have faith was to be right with God – that is, to live in an attitude of trust in God. Faith is the right way to live in the sight of God. It may therefore be helpful to paraphrase the word *justification*, perhaps as 'a state of being right with God'. Similarly, 'to be justified' could be paraphrased as 'to be put in a right relationship with God'.

Not only is the phrase 'justification by faith' unfamiliar; it is also open to misunderstanding. The phrase might appear to mean that we are justified *on account of our faith*. In other words, human faith is the basis of God's decision to grant us the status of being righteous in his sight. If this were the case, this would amount to a doctrine of justification by works, with faith being seen merely as a special type of good work. Faith would be something we achieve.

In fact, the phrase 'justification by faith' has a quite different meaning, which is perhaps best understood by considering a Latin phrase the German Reformer Philipp Melanchthon (1497–1560) used in explaining it. We are justified *propter Christum per fidem* – that is, on account of Christ, through faith. The basis of God's decision to place us in a right relationship with him lies in Jesus Christ himself. We are justified on account of his obedience during his lifetime and his death upon the cross. It is because of him, and not because of anything we have done or will do, that we are made right with God. But the means by which we are justified is faith. Faith is like a channel through which the benefits of Christ flow to us.

We are not justified *on account of* faith; we are justified *through* faith. It is the work of Christ, not our faith, that is the foundation of justification. Faith is the means by which the work of Christ is applied to our lives. This is no doctrine of justification on account of human achievement; it is a doctrine of justification on account of what Christ has achieved for us through his cross and resurrection. It is faith in Christ, not faith in our own faith, that places us in a right relationship with God.

But the doctrine implies still more than this. Faith is itself a gift of God.

In other words, both the external foundation and the internal means of appropriation of justification are God-given. Faith is not something we can achieve; it is something achieved within us by God. This assertion might seem bewildering if faith is simply understood as 'assent to the existence of God', or 'belief in the key doctrines of Christianity'. However, the full Christian understanding of faith embraces far more than this. Faith unites us to Christ and all his benefits. Everything necessary for salvation has been done, and done well, by God.

So how does the doctrine of justification by faith relate to self-esteem? The key linking concept is that of *righteousness*. For the Christian, it may be helpful to think of positive self-esteem as a psychological sign of having comprehended that one is counted as right with God, and thus with oneself.

Earlier, we noted a distinction between internal and external styles of attribution in relation to self-esteem. The Greek verb translated 'to justify' really has the sense 'to count someone as righteous', or 'to esteem someone as righteous'. There are two quite different ways of thinking about the idea of being justified in the sight of God. The first way involves an internal style of attribution, in which the following question is asked: 'What is it about *me* that would allow anyone to count *me* as righteous?' This way of thinking can lead to despair if the person's self-view is negative, and to an unmerited conceit if the person holds a good opinion of himself or herself.

The internal-attribution style naturally leads to the triumphalist view that we can do something to establish our righteousness. If we can justify ourselves by works (the Pelagian idea), our emotional investment tends to fall on our achievements and spurs us on to attempt to achieve more. Our sense of personal security and esteem thus comes to rest upon what we do and the way we feel about it.

The second approach concerns an external style of attribution, in which the question being asked is: 'What is it about *God* that makes him see me as righteous?' This style of attribution creates a sense of expectancy for action on the part of God, rather than a feeling that *we* ought to be achieving something. This vital shift in the frame of reference moves us away from a human-centred, works-orientated approach to our personal worth, and instead points us firmly towards a God-centred, faith-orientated approach.

(As we noted earlier, 'faith' does not mean a human work, but a work or gift of God within us.)

Justification is thus about our status in the sight of God. It is about the way we are viewed by that most significant of all others – God. The Greek word translated 'righteousness' is not simply a moral idea. It is far more than that, embracing central Christian ideas such as 'being in a right relationship with God' and 'being regarded as of worth by God'. Believers thus regard themselves (rightly!) as sinners; but in the sight of God, they are also righteous on account of their justification. God reckons believers as righteous on account of their faith. Through faith, the believer is clothed with the righteousness of Christ, in much the same way, Luther suggests, as Ezekiel 16:8 speaks of God covering our nakedness with his garment. For Luther, faith is the right (or righteous) relationship to God. Sin and righteousness thus coexist; we remain sinners inwardly, but we are righteous extrinsically in the sight of God. By confessing our sins in faith, we stand in a right and righteous relationship with God. From our own perspective we are sinners; but in the perspective of God we are righteous.

> Now the saints are always aware of their sin and seek righteousness from God in accordance with his mercy. And for this very reason, they are regarded as righteous by God. Thus in their own eyes (and in reality!) they are sinners – but in the eyes of God they are righteous, because he reckons them as such on account of their confession of their sin. In reality they are sinners; but they are righteous by the imputation of a merciful God. They are unknowingly righteous, and knowingly sinners. They are sinners in fact, but righteous in hope (Luther, *Commentary on Romans* 4:8).

Luther is not necessarily implying that this co-existence of sin and righteousness is a permanent condition. His point is that God shields our sin through his righteousness. His righteousness is like a protective covering under which we may battle with our sin. But *the existence of sin does not negate our status as Christians*. In justification, we are given the status of righteousness, while we work with God towards attaining the nature of righteousness. In that God has promised to make us righteous one day, finally eliminating our sin, there is a sense in which we are already righteous in his sight.

This way of thinking is important in a pastoral context. A colleague once described a meeting he had attended at his local church, dealing with the theme of self-esteem. All were asked to rate themselves on a scale between zero (terrible) and ten (perfect). Most of those people rated themselves between four and six (not especially good, but not especially bad either). The visiting speaker (who had been reading some fashionable works of psychotherapy) then declared that they all ought to rate themselves as ten; they were, he said, all perfect and merely suffered from a lack of self-esteem. This provoked an amused reaction among those present, who regarded their self-estimation as accurate and that of their speaker as hopelessly optimistic and deluded.

This incident brings out neatly the reluctance on the part of many modern persons to accept the fact that they are less than perfect. To concede imperfection seems tantamount to a humiliating and degrading admission of total failure. This denial of sin finds its natural expression in the myth of perfection – the unrealistic belief that the way we are is the way we are meant to be. The doctrine of justification invites us to acknowledge our imperfection and sin – while rejoicing in the purpose and power of God to transform the poverty of our nature into the likeness of Jesus Christ.

The story also illustrates how important, helpful and *Christian* Luther's approach to this problem of self-esteem turns out to be. God accepts us as we are. We do not have to rate ourselves at ten to be good Christians. Nor is perfection a prerequisite of acceptance in the sight of God. God accepts us just as we are; he grants us the status of ten on account of his promise to renew and refashion us totally. We score four, five, or six – but we are none the less accepted in his graciousness. We don't have to delude ourselves (or think God is deluded) by pretending we are perfect.

The justification of sinners rests upon no delusions, no legal fictions, and no pretence of holiness. God accepts us for what we are, while he works within us what he wants us to be. We are given the *status* of ten in the light of God's promise to rebuild us and finally to give us the *nature* of ten. And that gives us encouragement and motivation to move up the scale, receiving his strength and nature in place of our weaknesses and shortcomings. And so, by the grace of God, our fours, fives or sixes become eights, nines or tens. God grants us now a status that reflects his vision, intention and promise concerning what we shall be when recreated by his grace.

But now consider the approach of our amateur psychotherapist. He was telling his hearers that they were perfect. They considered his assessment ludicrous for two reasons. First, it did not accord with their experience. Whatever pretence of perfection they chose to maintain in public, in private they were perfectly aware of their sin. And second, it removed any motivation for self-improvement or growth in holiness. If one scores ten out of ten, there is nothing more to achieve. Luther's approach avoids both these pitfalls. It declares that we *are* sinners (which resonates with our own experience and knowledge of ourselves) and that there is considerable room for improvement. But it also affirms that we have the status of being righteous in the sight of God.

An awareness of sin, then, is not necessarily a symptom of lapse from faith or a sign of imperfect commitment to God. It can be nothing more than a reflection of the continuing struggle against sin, which is an essential component of justification and renewal. Let Luther have the final word on this point:

> In ourselves, we are sinners, and yet through faith we are righteous by the imputation of God. For we trust him who promises to deliver us, and in the meantime struggle so that sin may not overwhelm us, but that we may stand up to it until he finally takes it away from us (*Commentary on Romans* 4:7–8).

Earlier we pointed out that self-esteem entails elements of both judgment and emotion. In a similar way, being put in a right relationship with God entails both the objective truth of what Christ has achieved for us on the cross and the subjective experience of entering into a *relationship* with God. In the present chapter, we have been exploring how the cross of Christ establishes our righteousness in the sight of God. We now consider the way this change in status is experienced in the life of the believer. Earlier the theme of reconciliation was introduced. It is no accident that Jesus chose to illustrate this theme with a story of a wayward son who is restored to his father (Luke 15:11–24):

'[The son] got up and went to his father.

But while he was still a long way off, his father saw him and was filled with compassion for him; he ran to his son, threw his arms around him and kissed him.

The son said to him, "Father, I have sinned against heaven and against you. I am no longer worthy to be called your son."

But the father said to his servants, "Quick! Bring the best robe and put it on him. Put a ring on his finger and sandals on his feet. Bring the fattened calf and kill it. Let's have a feast and celebrate. For this son of mine was dead and is alive again; he was lost and is found"' (Luke 15:20–24).

So what does it mean to experience the fatherhood of God? What are the implications of that experience for self-esteem?

6

The parental care of God

Father God, I wonder how I managed to exist
Without the knowledge of Your parenthood
And Your loving care.
But now I am your son,
I am adopted in Your family
And I can never be alone,
'Cause, Father God, you're there beside me.

Ian Smale

In an earlier chapter, we drew attention to the importance of parental attachment for self-esteem. Positive self-esteem is seen to be linked with attachment to parents or significant others; negative self-esteem appears to be linked with separation from such people. As we have already hinted, the Christian understanding of God's parental care has much to say here. The fatherhood of God, linked with some strongly maternal scriptural images, suggests that Christian self-esteem should be grounded in our attachment to God through Christ.

We could compare this with some secular approaches to self-esteem as follows:

- *Cognitive behaviour therapy*: looking *outwards* towards goals, achievements, successes, and the meaning we give them in our lives
- *Client-centred psychotherapy*: looking *inwards* towards ourselves, stripped of spurious external assessments
- *Christianity*: looking *upwards* towards God and the risen Christ

Paul expresses the importance of this 'looking upwards' when he writes:

Since, then, you have been raised with Christ, set your hearts on things above, where Christ is seated at the right hand of God. Set your minds on things above, not on earthly things. For you died, and your life is now hidden with Christ in God (Col. 3:1–3).

Our longing for the Father

Because we have been created by God, we shall remain unfulfilled without him. This notion underlies the famous words of Augustine, framed as a prayer to God: 'You have made us for yourself, and our hearts are restless until they rest in you.' The doctrines of creation and redemption combine to interpret this sense of dissatisfaction and lack of fulfilment as a loss – a loss of fellowship with God – which can be restored. They yield a picture of a broken human nature, which still possesses an ability to be aware of its loss and to hope that it might be restored. Yet human nature is unable to satisfy itself by its own devices. As Blaise Pascal put it, there is a God-shaped void within us, which nothing else will ever fill. Our sense of emptiness is actually a sense of the absence of God from lives which were fashioned in his image

According to Augustine, we experience a sense of separation from the presence of God. He expressed this idea beautifully when he spoke of the 'loving memory' of God. It is a *memory* of God that is grounded in the doctrines of creation and redemption, which affirm that we have partially *lost* something through sin – and are somehow made aware of that loss through grace. It is a *loving* memory in that it is experienced as a sense of divine nostalgia, of spiritual wistfulness. We long to be reattached to God, to cleave to him once more and have our enforced separation from him ended.

The gospel declares that God has ended this enforced separation by breaking the power of that which enforced it – sin. The cross of Christ marks the end of the reign of sin. Our isolation from God is ended by that cross. Matthew records an incident of vital importance to our theme of self-esteem. At the moment of Christ's death, the temple curtain was torn asunder (Matt. 27:51). The curtain symbolized the remoteness and distance of God from his people; none save the high priest were allowed to venture past that curtain. That barrier is now removed. There is no longer any enforced separation from God.

It is for reasons such as this that the cross is, and must be, the ultimate grounds of Christian confidence. The cross establishes restoration to fellowship with God and access to his presence. 'Let us then approach the throne of grace with confidence, so that we may receive mercy and find grace' (Heb. 4:16). Through the cross of Christ, we are restored to fellowship with our Father God, with all the benefits that this brings to us.

But speaking of God as Father raises a different problem for others. Might not our faith in God as Father be nothing more than a projection of our secret longing for a father or mother from whom we have become separated? Is the idea of God as a father simply some kind of wish fulfilment? Is our sense of the existence of a heavenly Father nothing more than a secret hope that our greatest longings might be fulfilled? Is God for real – or is he just an illusion, like a dream in the night?

Yet if we are indeed created in the image and likeness of God (Gen. 1:26–27), is it so surprising that we should wish to relate to him? Might not a human desire for God be grounded in the fact that he brought us into being for the purpose of relating to him and with an inbuilt capacity to do so? After all, the first major insight encountered in Scripture is that God created the world. Is it therefore surprising that this creation should bear witness to him? Or that the height of his creation, human nature, should carry a recognizable imprint of his nature? And that this imprint might have considerable value as a starting point for apologetics? Paul believed passionately in the theological truth and apologetic importance of this insight (Rom. 1 – 2).

Furthermore, the parables of Jesus stress the ability of human relationships to mirror our relation to God. Human fatherhood, however inadequately, can point to the fatherhood of God and give substance and meaning to what might otherwise degenerate into an abstract idea.

Through the grace of God, the creation is able to point to its Creator. Through the generosity of God, we have been left with a latent memory of him, capable of stirring us to recollect him in his fullness. Although there is a fracture, a disjuncture, between the ideal and the empirical, between the realms of fallen and redeemed creation, the memory of that connection lives on, along with the intimation of its restoration through redemption.

Belonging to the Father

To be a Christian is to belong to God our Father. So what difference does this make? And how does this impact upon self-esteem? In what follows, we shall explore a number of aspects of 'belonging to the Father' which help us appreciate the centrality of this idea to the issue of self-esteem.

Family resemblance

All of us resemble our biological parents in some ways. We inherit both desirable and undesirable characteristics. As we know to our cost, nothing annoys adolescents more than comments such as 'He's a chip off the old block', or 'She's the image of her mother.' We inherit physical features, such as hair colour, abilities and characteristic ways of behaving. Scripture stresses that all human beings are also, and primarily, made in the image of God (Gen. 1:26–27). This means that, like God, we have the capacity and desire to create and to love. We are not just made by God; we have something of God's nature in us. This is why, when we look at other human beings, we should be able to see God in them (1 John 4:20). In this sense the idea of God as our Father goes beyond that of God as our Creator. We are not just his handiwork; we are his offspring.

Gaining a pedigree

Earlier we noted how self-esteem is related to pedigree. Important family connections, and especially the idea of having a status that goes back centuries, boost our sense of worth. The image of the fatherhood of God, especially as this relates to adoption, affirms that, as members of the family of God, we share in a distinguished pedigree going back to the dawn of time.

In the New Testament Paul explores this aspect of self-esteem through faith as he stresses that Abraham is the spiritual forebear of all those who put their trust in God. All those who share his faith may look back to him as their forebear and gain a sense of personal dignity and worth as a result. The promise to Abraham – that he would have countless descendants – embraces all those who, like us, have trusted in the promises of a trustworthy God. We can imagine a family tree of faith that traces the people through whom each of us came to faith. In the end, that family tree will include Abraham as the father of all who believe.

Naming is an important aspect of gaining a pedigree. To become a member of the family of God is to be called by the name of Christian. Scripture gives many instances of people being given names as a token of their new and closer relationship with God. Abram becomes Abraham; Sarai becomes Sarah; Simon becomes Peter; Saul becomes Paul. A new name symbolizes a new relationship of belonging.

A common theme to be found in the traditional tales of many cultures is that of the changeling prince. The hero is someone of low social status, such as a peasant or working-class youth. This person has low self-esteem. But, unknown to him, he is a changeling. At the time of his birth, he had been swapped with another infant of high social status. Often the story portrays the midwife to a royal household substituting her own infant child for the royal baby in order that her child may enjoy a regal lifestyle. And so the changeling prince grows up, believing himself to be of peasant stock, unaware that he is of royal descent. Then, often in a moment of high drama, he discovers his real identity. He is of royal descent! His self-valuation increases enormously as a result. (Examples of this storyline can be found in Verdi's *Il trovatore* and

Gilbert and Sullivan's *The Gondoliers*.)

That story in some shape or form is familiar to us all. Relating to the theme of Christian self-esteem, it shows the importance of our descent for self-value. Parents provide status for the child, a status which otherwise might never be possible. The Christian's status derives from God our Father, who has adopted us into his family through faith.

We need to appreciate that, through faith, we are of royal descent. We who were born of water are now born of the Spirit of God (John 3:5). We who were born mortal have been given the gift of eternal life. We who were born of earthly fathers have been born again into the family of God, with God as our Father.

Inheritance rights

For Paul, Christians are not simply the natural children of God, we are also adopted into the family of God through faith, given the legal status of adopted children and all that that entails. That 'spirit of sonship' brings with it full inheritance rights from our heavenly Father, so that all that Christ (as the natural Son of God) obtained from him will one day be ours as well. Thus Paul stresses that we who suffer with Christ will one day share in his risen glory on account of our common family links and inheritance privileges. We have been *chosen* to be members of the family of God, with all the privileges this entails.

If we have been adopted into the family of God, with God as our Father, we receive certain inheritance rights (Rom. 8:17). We are full heirs of God and co-heirs with Christ. To be a child of God is to be an heir of God. Martin Luther developed this important idea with reference to the word *testament* (as in New Testament). The word *testament*, Luther argues, is familiar to all through the idea of a last will and testament. It brings together three related ideas:

- the promise of the testator to bestow his estate upon his heirs
- the naming of those heirs
- the death of the testator in order that the inheritance may be given to the heirs

Luther's argument proceeds thus: God has promised an inheritance of forgiveness and eternal life. This inheritance is promised to all who turn to him in faith and believe in his promises of redemption. And, on account of the death of Jesus Christ, those promises are now open, and that inheritance is now available.

Fatherly care

God's fatherly care for his children meets their deepest needs: for nurture, acceptance, setting of clear standards, and teaching.

Nurture. Just as an earthly father cares for his children, so God knows our needs and meets them.

> '... do not worry about your life, what you will eat or drink; or about your body, what you will wear ... Who of you by worrying can add a single hour to his life?
>
> 'And why do you worry about clothes? See how the lilies of the field grow. They do not labour or spin. Yet I tell you that not even Solomon in all his splendour was dressed like one of these. If that is how God clothes the grass of the field, which is here today and tomorrow is thrown into the fire, will he not much more clothe you, O you of little faith? So do not worry, saying, "What shall we eat?" or "What shall we drink?" or "What shall we wear?"' (Matt. 6:25–31).

Acceptance. Unconditional acceptance is central to responsible parenting. Knowing that he or she is accepted provides a secure base from which the child can grow. God is a secure base, as the parable of the man who builds his house upon the rock (Matt. 7:24–27) makes clear. Just as the father rejoiced at the return of the prodigal son, so God accepts us unconditionally, even when we wander far from him (Luke 15:11–24).

Setting of clear standards. Fathers, while unconditionally accepting their children, nevertheless set clear limits to their behaviour. Acceptance is unconditional; that acceptance does not, however, preclude the setting out of well-defined behavioural expectations. We are called to be holy, as God is holy; we are called to standards of behaviour that are higher than those of the secular world.

Teaching. A central aspect of fatherly responsibility, and parental responsibility in general, is guidance and teaching. Hosea sets out one of the finest illustrations of God's guidance for his people: God holds his child Israel by the hand and leads him out of Egypt. Even though Israel rebelled against him, God continued to love his child. He bent down and fed Israel, nourishing his child (Hos. 11:1–4). Such is his love for his people Israel, even in their waywardness, that he could never give them up (Hos. 11:8).

Even earthly fathers, sinful though they are, care for their children. Jesus makes this point with force in the Sermon on the Mount:

> 'Which of you, if his son asks for bread, will give him a stone? Or if he asks for a fish, will give him a snake? If you, then, though you are evil, know how to give good gifts to your children, how much more will your Father in heaven give good gifts to those who ask him!' (Matt. 7:9–11).

The natural care of human fathers and mothers for their children reflects (and, as we shall see later, is grounded in) the nature of God himself. Time and time again, Scripture affirms God's love for his people, often using maternal images to do so.

> 'As a mother comforts her child,
>   so will I comfort you ...'
>
> (Is. 66:13)

> 'Can a mother forget the baby at her breast
>   and have no compassion on the child she has borne?
> Though she may forget,
>   I will not forget you!'
>
> (Is. 49:15)

The nature of God shines through his creation, however dimly, in the love of parents for those whom they have brought into being.

We have already noted the importance of the love of another for self-esteem. The fatherly care of God for his children is vital in this regard. Knowing that we are the children of God ought to mean knowing that we are the *loved* children of God. Anyone who has anxieties about this is invited to reflect upon the cross, where God achieves the salvation of his people at enormous cost to himself. Let us explore this further.

Think of how you might try to show someone that you love him or her. You might tell the person so; you might write it; you might visit the person; you might send flowers. The more the token of love demands of you, the more precious and convincing it is. It is therefore no wonder that the supreme act of love is to give your life for someone who matters to you. 'Greater love has no one than this, that he lay down his life for his friends' (John 15:13). In the death of Christ, we can see the overwhelming love of God for us. There was no limit to Christ's self-giving for us. His death marks his total self-giving in that act of love which redeems us. That is how much he values us. He gives everything he has and everything he is for us. That thought must allow us to walk tall, secure in the fatherly love of God.

Even though we are sinners, God loves us. There is no contradiction here. God loves us unconditionally. There is no delusion or deception here. As the psalmist stresses (Ps. 139:1–4), God knows exactly what we are like. He sees through us to the depths of our being. He knows that we are sinners – but loves us all the same. St Paul makes this point forcefully (Rom. 5:7–8). You can understand, he muses, why someone should want to give his life for someone really important or good. Yet Christ died to demonstrate his love for sinners. We are sinners who are loved and valued by God our Father.

The Father's pain

Attachment is a two-way process. In recent years research in attachment theory has come to focus on *parental* separation anxiety. The first day at 'big school' is often as difficult for parents as it is for the child. In a similar way God is pained by our separation from him. This is not the way he wishes it to be. He did not create us so to live apart from him. We are created by him and for him; the fact that we are alienated and estranged from him causes him suffering and pain. Jesus grieved over Jerusalem (Matt. 23:37–38), speaking of his longing to gather her children to himself.

The New Testament emphasizes the joy of the Father over the reconciliation of his children to fellowship with himself. He wants us to return to him. Luke 15 brings together three parables concerning lostness: a lost sheep (verses 3–7), a lost coin (verses 8–10) and a lost son (verses 11–32). And each of these parables has a common sequence: that which is lost is found, and all rejoice. Our reconciliation to God brings rejoicing in its wake. 'I tell you, there is rejoicing in the presence of the angels of God over one sinner who repents' (verse 10).

One of the finest explorations of the pain of the Father is found in the writings of the Japanese theologian Kazoh Kitamori (born 1916). In his work *The Pain of God*, which was published in the aftermath of the Second World War, Kitamori emphasizes how God shares in the suffering and pain of his creation. He is hurt by our pain and deeply moved by our sadness. The Father shares in our pain and grieves over his separation from us through sin. Similar ideas can be found in the writings of the German theologian Jürgen Moltmann (born 1926). In his book *The Crucified God*, Moltmann draws our attention to the pain which God suffers on account of the death of his Son. The Son suffers separation from his Father, and the Father suffers the loss of his Son. They are linked together by a common bond of suffering. We have already seen how Christ suffers both moral and physical separation from his Father at the time of his death. It is too easy to overlook the effect that the death of Christ has upon God himself. Moltmann asks us to appreciate the painful effect of the Father's separation from and loss of his Son.

A human picture of the Father's pain is given in biblical references to the anguish that Mary is called to endure at the death of her beloved Son (Luke 2:35; John 19:25). This theme is explored in some detail in the medieval poem 'Stabat Mater dolorosa' (the title of which means 'The mother stood weeping'), which is a vivid portrayal of the sorrow and grief of Mary as she watches Christ die on the cross.

Theological foundations of the fatherhood of God

Underlying all these observations, however, is a deeper issue of such theological importance that it must be addressed. How can we think of God as Father? What does it mean to speak of the 'fatherhood of God'? And what is the status of this relationship? In other words, how does God relate to our own fathers?

The basic theological principle involved here is known as the 'analogy of being', which is particularly well stated in the writings of the great thirteenth-century theologian Thomas Aquinas. We could summarize what Aquinas says along the following lines. God reveals himself in forms that relate to our everyday experience. On account of the frailty and limitations of our human intellects, God reveals himself in ways we can understand. He accommodates himself to our capacity.

An illustration will make this clearer. Consider the statement, 'God is our Father.' Aquinas argues that this means that God is *like* a human father. In other words, God is analogous to a father. In some ways he is like a human father, and in others he is not. There are genuine points of similarity. God cares for us, as human fathers care for their children (note Matt. 7:9–11). God is the ultimate source of our existence, just as our fathers brought us into being. He exercises authority over us, as do human fathers. Equally, there are genuine points of dissimilarity. God is not a human being, for example. Nor does the necessity of both a human father and a mother in procreation indicate the need for a divine father and a divine mother.

The idea that Aquinas is trying to convey is clear. God reveals himself in images and ideas that tie in with our everyday existence – yet which do not reduce God to the level of that everyday world. When we say that 'God is our Father', we don't mean that he is just another human father. Rather, we mean that thinking about human fathers helps us think about God. This is an analogy. Like all analogies, it breaks down in places. However, analogies are still extremely useful and vivid ways of thinking about God.

Why is the use of analogy so important? First, analogies high-light God's ability to reveal himself in ways we can understand. The scriptural images of God (for example, as shepherd, king and father) are deceptively simple. They are easy to visualize and re-member; yet on further reflection, they convey important and profound truths concerning God. The doctrine of the incarnation speaks of God's willingness and ability to come down to our level. God reveals himself in ways appropriate to our level and our capacity as human beings, using illustrations we can handle. It is easy to think about God as a shepherd or a father. Yet this doesn't mean that God *is* a shepherd or that God *is* a human father. That would be to reduce God to a purely human level. Rather, qualities of shepherds and human fathers help us to understand what God is like. God is *like* a shepherd or a human father. These images are not *identical* with God, yet are *analogous* with him. Analogies mean that God is revealed in our terms, without being reduced to our level.

Secondly, analogies are memorable. They are powerful visual images that make a direct and powerful appeal to our imagination. We all know that a picture is worth a thousand words. It is theologically correct to talk about God as one who cares for us, guides us and accompanies us throughout life. But it is much more memorable to talk about God as a shepherd – an analogy which makes all those points. People can remember the idea of God as a shepherd, linking it with key scriptural passages (such as Ps. 23). And as they think about those images, they can begin to unpack the various ideas these convey.

The parables Jesus himself told are classic illustrations of this process. These parables are vivid images of everyday life, which act as windows through which we can catch a glimpse of God. Com-plicated ideas – such as forgiveness, or the co-existence of good and evil in the world – are presented in simple pictures. The parables in no way reduce God to the level of the natural world. They demonstrate God's ability and determination to reveal himself in ways we can remember and understand. It is a concession to our human frailty and weakness, which God knows and understands.

Scripture gives us a range of images when it describes God. These images interact, modifying each other and limiting the range of interpretations we can place upon them. An example of how images interact may make this clearer. Take the analogies of king, father and shepherd. Each of these three analogies conveys the idea of authority, fundamental to our understanding of God. Kings, however, often behave in arbitrary ways which are not always in the best interests of their subjects. The analogy of God as a king might thus be misunderstood to suggest that God is some sort of tyrant. However, Scripture speaks of God showing the tender compassion of a father towards his children (Ps. 103:13–18) and the total dedication of a good shepherd to the welfare of his flock (John 10:11). His authority is exercised tenderly and wisely.

Of course, the analogy works the other way as well. Earthly rulers, fathers and pastors are meant to model their conduct after the likeness of God, who sets the example. Rulers should be persons of total integrity and dedication, committed to the well-being of their people. Fathers should exercise authority over their children with kindness and compassion. Pastors should demonstrate tenderness and dedication towards those committed to their care. Analogies thus help us to think about God and also about the way God would like his world to be.

This two-way relationship between human analogy and divine reality avoids an important difficulty. Many people find the idea of God as Father unhelpful, on account of their negative experience with their own fathers: 'If God is like my father, I don't want anything to do with him.' Some human fathers are simply tyrants or abusers; the image of God this suggests is both unattractive and untrue. Certain human fathers are found wanting in the light of what Scripture suggests fatherhood should include. Scripture commends certain patterns of fatherhood, in the first place as models for human fathers to imitate and, in the second, to govern our thinking about God himself. While all fathers may mirror God to some extent, some reflect God considerably better than others.

The idea lying behind Aquinas's doctrine of analogy, then, is of fundamental importance to the way we think about God. It illuminates the manner in which God reveals himself to us through Scripture. It helps us understand how God can be *above* our world and yet simultaneously reveal himself *in* that world. God is not an object or a person in space and time; nevertheless, such persons and objects can help us to deepen our appreciation of who God is and what he is like. God, who is infinite, is able to express himself reliably and adequately in human words and finite images. Yet, as

Aquinas stressed, no contradiction is involved. There is thus no fundamental difficulty in using the image of God as Father in this way.

7

Content in all circumstances: the redeemed life

> I consider everything a loss compared to the surpassing greatness of knowing Christ Jesus my Lord, for whose sake I have lost all things. I consider them rubbish, that I may gain Christ and be found in him (Phil. 3:8–9).

We have already explored some of the ways in which Christian confidence is grounded in the cross of Christ. In order to give more substance to this approach, we now turn to one writing in the New Testament which is of especial interest in this context – Paul's letter to the Philippians. In many ways this letter can be regarded as an extended commentary on the foundations and consequences of proper Christian self-esteem.

One of the most remarkable features of this letter is its affirming nature. Many of Paul's letters are written to counter false teaching in the churches. An example is the letter to the Galatians, in which Paul challenges the teaching that justification comes about through works of the law. The letter to the Philippians, however, is purely positive in tone. Throughout this letter, Paul affirms his readers and himself in the service of God and his gospel. The letter is packed with insights of vital relevance to Christian self-esteem.

The letter to the Philippians

Although it is one of the shortest of his writings, Paul's letter to the church at Philippi is widely regarded as one of the most moving of the New Testament writings. It is one of Paul's later letters, probably written from Rome at some point in the period AD 60–64. That it was written from Rome is suggested by a number of features of the letter, such as the reference to the 'palace' or the 'palace guard' (1:13) and to 'Caesar's household' (4:22). There are some grounds for thinking that the letter may have been written a little earlier from the city of Ephesus (perhaps at some point around AD 55–57), although the majority opinion among scholars still seems to favour the view that the letter was written from Rome towards the end of Paul's life.

What of Philippi? The city was located in Macedonia close to neighbouring Thrace. In modern terms, this means that the site of Philippi is to be found in north-eastern Greece, not far from the Turkish border. Philippi was founded as the city of Krenides by an Athenian exile, Callistratus. The city was refounded as a Roman colony after Anthony and Octavian defeated Brutus and Cassius in 42/41 BC. This battle, which marked the end of the Roman Republic, has been made immortal by Shakespeare's famous lines in *Julius Caesar*: 'I will see thee at Philippi, then.'

After the defeat of Anthony's forces at Actium eleven years later, the Emperor Octavian reconstituted the colony once more. The city thus developed a decidedly Italian atmosphere on account of both the permanent presence of Italian settlers and the large numbers of Roman troops regularly passing through the city because of its strategic location in Macedonia. The language, imagery and outlooks of a Roman colony would thus be part of the everyday thinking of Paul's audience within the city. Philippi was conscious of its ties with Rome, including its language (Latin seems to have been more widely spoken than Greek) and laws. Roman institutions served as the model in many areas of its communal life.

This chapter is not a detailed commentary on the letter, which would merit a far more extended analysis. Rather, we set out to pick up some themes important to Christian self-esteem, and to indicate how helpful these can be to Christians troubled by a radical lack of self-worth.

Slaves and saints: anxieties about personal worth

The letter opens with a salutation from Paul and Timothy, who identify themselves as 'servants of Christ Jesus' (1:1). The Greek word used here is probably better translated as 'slave'. The great paradox of faith is that we find our perfect freedom only when we become slaves – slaves to God. Christians have been freed from slavery to sin and the fear of death, and brought into the glorious liberty of the children of God. The death of Christ is the price paid to purchase this freedom.

Nestling within the phrase 'slaves of Christ Jesus' is a wonderful insight. In the ancient world, slaves judged their status in relation to the importance of their masters. The greater the social status of a master, the greater the esteem of the slave. Christians are slaves of the greatest and kindest Master of all, the present ruler and judge of the world. They have been set free from bondage to inferior authorities (such as sin, death and the world) in order that they may serve Christ, and are able to exult in the new status that this brings.

The letter is addressed 'to all the saints in Christ Jesus at Philippi' (1:1). The use of the word 'saints' raises a number of important questions for self-esteem. In what way can we think of Christians as saints when they are so obviously sinners as well? Groucho Marx once remarked that he wouldn't want to join a club that would have him as a member. Many Christians feel that way about the idea of saints. If we are all saints, the word seems to be devalued. How can we, who are conscious of our sins and failings, be thought of as saints?

Yet we are saints, not because of any holiness on our part, but on account of the holiness of the one who calls us. God doesn't call those who are already holy (as if these existed); he calls those who are sinners (Mark 2:17), and are prepared to admit it. Yet because of God's total faithfulness to his promises, those who are now sinners may rejoice in the quiet confidence of faith, knowing that God, having begun a good work in them, will see it through to completion (Phil. 1:6). It is our grasp upon the living God, not our present holiness, that is of vital importance in this respect.

We can look forward with confidence to being able to stand among the company of saints on the last day – not due to our merit, but due to God's faithfulness to his promises. Yet our present self-esteem is enormously enhanced by the knowledge of our future status. We are like a youth who, although presently poor, knows that he will enter into an inheritance when he reaches the age of majority. He is able to live in hope and dignity in the knowledge of what is stored up for him in the future. And so we who are Christians can look forward with confidence and eager anticipation to what lies ahead of us and begin to savour it now.

Paul opens his letter with a strongly affirming statement. He remembers the Christians at Philippi with thankfulness and joy (1:3). He longs for them and yearns to be with them (1:8). They matter to him. Christians who read this letter can share in this affirmation. They share the same faith and commitment as their Philippian predecessors. We share with Paul in the partnership of the gospel. We, in our own day and age, continue the work he began nearly two thousand years ago. There is a sense of honour and personal worth associated with this major insight. We have been called to share in a vitally important task.

Paul in chains: content in all circumstances

Paul now moves on (1:12–30) to speak of his own situation. He is in prison. For many, that would result in a serious loss of self-esteem. In the eyes of the world, being imprisoned amounted to a loss of personal dignity. Part of the deterrent value of imprisonment was the shame it brought to both the prisoner and his family. Yet Paul is able to find meaning and dignity in his situation. He is 'in chains for Christ' (1:13), and his guards know this.

This point can be reinforced by considering the shame of Christ upon the cross. Christ endured the shame and public humiliation of the events which led up to his execution. The public scourging, the mocking of the crowd, the casting of lots for his pitiful possessions – in every respect, Christ was put to shame by the manner of his death.

It is not the *situation* that determines our self-esteem; it is what we allow God to do through it. Paul's testimony brings home that God is able to use people in situations the world regards as humiliating and degrading. Christians are able to find dignity and comfort in whatever situation they find themselves, through knowing that God will be able to use them in those situations.

Considerations such as this enable Paul not merely to cope with such situations, but to rejoice in them (1:18–20). Christian faith means a sure and firm confidence that, whatever happens, God will be able to use us. Some Christians devalue themselves totally. They may believe that they are utterly useless and that God could do nothing with them or through them. Or they may think that they have landed themselves in a situation that prevents them from having an effective Christian ministry. It may be that they failed to get the position they hoped for and have had to accept a post that seems vastly inferior, presenting fewer opportunities for effective ministry. And they feel utterly useless and valueless as a result.

Paul has important things to say to any who feel that way. First, the public valuation of one's position does not necessarily bear any relation to God's perception of things. As Paul reminded the Christians at Corinth (1 Cor. 1:26–29), God chose what the world regarded as weak and foolish in order to show how utterly spurious the world's standards are. It is not the world's valuation of things that matters, but God's. The world regarded prison as degrading and humiliating; Paul made it an effective arena for the proclamation of the gospel. We need to learn to see things through God's eyes, rather than through our own.

Secondly, self-devaluation is one of the most effective ways of preventing God from doing anything through us. Insisting that we are of no value is not simply false modesty; it is an insult to God. It implies that he has given us nothing. It amounts to a radical denial of his generosity. Paul does not say that Christians are devoid of gifts or talents; he simply insists that we see these gifts and talents in their proper light. 'What do you have that you did not receive? And if you did receive it, why do you boast as though you did not?' (1 Cor. 4:7). They are not rewards, reflecting our merits or achievements; they are gifts, reflecting the generosity of the giving God.

This same point is made by the parable of the talents (Matt.

25:14–30), which tells us that God has given all his people talents, not only as an expression of his generosity, but also because these are meant to be used to build up his church and extend his kingdom. And a crass denial of talent denies God the opportunity to work through us. A responsible Christian attitude involves recognizing that God has given all his people gifts. The false modesty that declares, 'I am nothing! I have no talents', blinds us to the very real gifts God has already given us and expects us to use. This false modesty encourages us to bury and deny talent. Yet God wants us to discover and use the gifts he has given us.

To value ourselves is to become receptive to what God has given us and to what he wants to make of us. A proper Christian self-esteem opens the door to discovering the many gifts God has already given us and wants us to use in serving him in his world and his church. Not all gifts are the same or of equal value. But our task is not to worry about what *other* people have been given, but to discover what we have been given. To become preoccupied with the talents of others is to become vulnerable to envy and can perpetuate low self-esteem. Instead, we should concentrate upon what we have been given and what this might be telling us about what we ought to be doing in God's service.

The humility of the believer

This naturally leads us to a discussion of Christian humility, which Paul explores at some length in Philippians 2:1–11. Humility can too often become little more than self-pitying introspection. The essence of humility does not lie in self-deprecation or devaluation, but in the positive evaluation of others. 'In humility count others better than yourselves' (2:3). Humility is not about lowering our valuation of ourselves, but about raising our valuation of others. We have already seen that one essential component of Christian humility is the recognition that all that we have and are comes from God. A second component is an awareness of how much God has given to others and a willingness to respect and celebrate this generosity to them.

Carl Rogers and others have argued that people cannot value others until they have learned to value themselves. There are strong indications of this approach in the New Testament. In urging us to love others as we love ourselves (Matt. 22:35–40; see Gal. 5:14), Jesus appears to assume that we *do* value ourselves – and that we can thus value others to the same extent. Indeed, the fact that God loves and values us is treated as the basis for the demand that we should love others to the same extent. 'Dear friends, since God so loved us, we also ought to love one another' (1 John 4:11). A real attachment to God is thus seen as leading to a natural desire to value others.

This might lead to envy, but Paul suggests that it can and should lead to humility. We should not be jealous of what God has given to others, but should rejoice over what he has given to us and ensure that we make full use of it. It also encourages us to realize that God bestows his gifts over the whole church, which is thus better equipped to serve the people of God. The gifts God entrusts to us find their full meaning and application in the context of the church.

The humility of Christ

Paul then moves on to explore the implications of the incarnation – the coming of Christ Jesus to this world in the form of a human being. Christ, Paul reminds his readers, 'made himself nothing, taking the very nature of a servant, being made in human likeness' (2:7). The theological implications of this are enormous and would require a book in its own right to explore them in the depth that they deserve. Our attention here, however, centres on its implications for Christian self-esteem.

Paul remarks that Jesus Christ, who was 'in the form of God' (2:6, mg.), became just like believers – a 'servant' (again, the Greek word really means 'slave') and appeared 'in human likeness'. In other words, in terms of his status and his nature, Christ became just like one of us. Christian theology makes much of the voluntary humiliation of Christ at this point. In order to achieve our salvation, Christ set aside his majesty and glory to become like one of us. But this has important ramifications for Christian self-esteem. Christ deems us worth saving. By becoming like us, he has brought new dignity to human nature. By humbling himself, Christ has raised us up. Our self-esteem must reflect this fact:

Christ valued us so much that he came among us, as one of us, content to share every aspect of our life, death included (2:7–8). And by exalting him (2:9), God has also exalted us. Through faith, we share in everything that Christ is and has.

The key point here is that Christ chose to set aside his majesty and status, in order to save us. We must appreciate what Christ gave up for us if we are to fully grasp the wonder of his love for us. He chose to humble himself, and to enter into this world as a slave, rather than as its rightful master and Lord. He who was rich beyond all splendour became poor for our sake. As Charles Wesley's famous hymn 'And Can It Be?' puts it:

> He left his Father's throne above, –
> So free, so infinite his grace, –
> Emptied himself of all but love,
> And bled for Adam's helpless race …

Christ was entitled to honour and glory; he chose to set it on one side, in order to become a servant. We must never think of this in terms of Christ's putting up with something undignified, or making the best of a bad situation. Christ insisted that servanthood was to be seen as the highest of callings, and demonstrated this by taking on this status himself. Incarnation is about both the affirmation and the embodiment of the values of the kingdom of God in Christ. When some of Christ's disciples fought over who would have the privilege of sitting at his right hand in the kingdom, Christ rebuked them by insisting that servanthood was the supreme privilege (Mark 10:44–45). By washing his disciples' feet shortly before his betrayal (John 15), Christ demonstrated the new status he had assigned to servanthood.

By becoming a slave, Christ affirmed the royal role of servanthood within the Christian community, and also manifested his commitment to believers. The full wonder of the extent to which God values us can be appreciated only when we recognize what the incarnation and crucifixion really mean. God humbles himself and stoops down to meet us where we are. Paul asks his readers to model that same humility in their dealings with each other.

So the Lord became a slave for us. This insight holds the key to a Christian understanding of humility. Christ stooped down to meet us, gladly lowering himself to where we are, so that he might raise us to where he is. It is only by reflecting on the full extent of Christ's humility – his entering into this world as a slave, suffering rejection and dying, rejected, on a cross – that we can even begin to grasp how much he loves us, and wants us to be with him.

Yet there is another aspect of this story. By becoming a slave for us, Christ confers his dignity on this role. We who are slaves for Christ can know that Christ has brought a new dignity and meaning to the concept. A slave is no longer a despised and reviled person. By becoming a slave, Christ brings a new sense of nobility and honour to this role. To be a slave for Christ is both a privilege and honour. The world may find difficulty in accepting this; for believers, it is a precious insight into the incarnation.

Blessings, not achievements: contrasting ideas of self-esteem

In the third chapter of Philippians, Paul contrasts an earthly notion of self-esteem – based upon national privilege, family background, and personal achievement – with an authentically Christian self-esteem based upon faith in Christ. Paul spends some time setting out his own credentials as a Jew (3:4–6). If self-esteem is based upon human considerations, he argues, then his credentials are impeccable. He was not merely a totally orthodox Jew, but one of Judaism's most distinguished representatives. Within the Jewish nation his standing was high. He would have been entitled to places of honour at the feasts and held in respect by his fellow-Jews. He was a Pharisee – both an honour and a considerable achievement for a Jew. By purely human standards, Paul's stock was high. If his valuation of himself rested upon his family and his achievements, then Paul's self-esteem was sky high. 'If anyone else thinks he has reasons to put confidence in the flesh, I have more' (3:4).

Yet Paul rejects all of this as spurious. 'But whatever was to my profit I now consider loss for the sake of Christ. What is more, I consider everything a loss compared to the surpassing greatness of knowing Christ Jesus my Lord, for whose sake I have lost all things' (3:7–8). Christian self-esteem is not based upon any national privilege, family entitlement or personal accomplishment. It is based solely and totally upon what God has done for us in Jesus Christ. Our self-esteem is something that God achieves for us, not something that we achieve for ourselves apart from God.

The fifteenth-century writer Thomas à Kempis once wrote that in the light of the cross of Christ all this world has to offer will fade into insignificance. The believer is meant to meditate upon Christ. *Et sic transit gloria mundi* – and thus the glory of the world fades away. So it is with self-esteem. What humans count as important and valuable is shown up in its true light in the cross of Christ – including human ideas of personal value. The cross of Christ alone is a secure rock to which we can anchor true valuation and esteem of ourselves and others.

Paul develops this idea with special reference to the idea of 'righteousness'. For Paul, this term refers to far more than a moral idea. It denotes our standing in the sight of God, the value God places upon us. In a vitally important passage, Paul contrasts a bogus self-esteem, based upon works of the law, with a genuine self-esteem, based upon faith in Christ. Paul declares that he is prepared to lose everything 'and be found in him, not having a righteousness of my own that comes from the law, but that which is through faith in Christ' (3:9). The contrast is clear. On the one hand, there is a righteousness based upon law – upon personal achievement or upon the Jewish law as a charter of national privilege. On this understanding of personal value, our self-esteem rests upon being a member of the Jewish nation, having rigorously kept each and every precept of the law, or having achieved a senior position within the social or religious hierarchy. Paul rejects this vigorously.

On the other hand, there is a righteousness 'which is through faith in Christ'. This is not a righteousness that we accomplish, but a righteousness that has been accomplished for us and is offered to us through faith. Faith is the channel that links us to Christ and all that he has achieved for us.

This contrast is brought out especially clearly by one of the most famous parables of the New Testament, told by Jesus to illustrate the difference between humanly constructed and divinely based valuations of oneself. Although it is very familiar, it is worth savouring the parable in its entirety:

'Two men went up to the temple to pray, one a Pharisee and the other a tax collector. The Pharisee stood up and prayed about himself: "God, I thank you that I am not like other men – robbers, evildoers, adulterers – or even like this tax collector. I fast twice a week and give a tenth of all I get."

'But the tax collector stood at a distance. He would not even look up to heaven, but beat his breast and said, "God, have mercy on me, a sinner."

'I tell you that this man, rather than the other, went home justified before God. For everyone who exalts himself will be humbled, and he who humbles himself will be exalted' (Luke 18:10–14).

Note that there is not the slightest suggestion that the Pharisee is a hypocrite. Christ takes him at face value. This Pharisee went beyond the demands of the law, which required him only to fast *once* a week and did not require him to give tithes (that is, 10%) of *all* of his incoming money and goods. The Pharisee, by fasting twice a week and giving tithes on all his income, exceeded the demands of the law.

Christ does not criticize the Pharisee for hypocrisy; there is no trace of any suggestion that the Pharisee's boasting was based on deception. The criticism Christ made was far more radical. The Pharisee placed his confidence in himself, rather than in God. His stance indicates this confidence: he feels able to stand upright in the presence of God, confident in – indeed, even proud of – his own achievements.

The tax collector, in total contrast, was not merely unwilling to stand in the presence of God; he even feels unable to draw near to God. He has no catalogue of achievements to rehearse. All he can do is confess that he is a sinner. Yet in his emptiness, he receives the fullness of God's grace, going home justified (that is, given the status of being righteous in the sight of God). His confidence is not in what he himself has achieved, but in the mercy and grace of God. Christ clearly commends this attitude, and we find Paul reflecting the 'mind of Christ' at this point.

As argued in an earlier section, this does not mean that we should devalue our achievements. Paul stresses that while achievements have no purchasing power on salvation, they are a proper response on our part to what God has done for us. The gospel liberates us from the oppressive mindset that declares: 'Unless you are perfect, you cannot be saved! Unless you are a high achiever, you cannot be saved! Unless you are a member of a privileged social group, you cannot be saved!' All that has been set firmly behind us. The gospel affirms that we have been set free from the delusion that we can buy our way into the presence of God. God has already come to us. To put this another way: we should not invest in externals, but rejoice in them.

Paul develops this point at greater length. Our self-esteem must not rest in what we think of ourselves, or in what other people think of us, but in what God thinks of us. The status with which God endows us is to be prized more greatly than anything the world can offer.

But Paul's argument is more fundamental than this. He suggests that the values of the world may prevent his readers from gaining Christ. The status the world accords to individuals and their actions may act as a barrier, preventing needy people from gaining Christ. The accumulation of achievements can divert us from building up a proper and robust self-esteem. Even those with a balanced self-esteem can see a better way reflected in God. Paul was glad to suffer the loss of everything because it led to the gain of something far greater – Christ himself. 'I consider everything a loss compared to the surpassing greatness of knowing Christ Jesus my Lord, for whose sake I have lost all things' (3:8). From the standpoint of one who has gained Christ, Paul is able to see how shallow and false those things were which once he had valued so highly. For Paul, the standards, values and outlook of the world are eclipsed by Christ. He alone is worth knowing, and his valuation alone is worth seeking.

Paul's point is this: to discover Christ is to delight in him and to esteem only what he values. It is to set aside worldly notions of self-esteem and self-value as inferior trinkets, which are totally eclipsed by the pearl of great price. Christ, and Christ alone, bestows dignity upon Christians, who are called by his name. All considerations of race, class, and personal achievement pale into insignificance in the light of Christ. The ultimate Christian privilege is 'to know Christ and the power of his resurrection' (3:10). This is not to devalue our achievements; it is simply to refuse to build our self-esteem upon them.

Christians have to learn that their value lies in their having been called and claimed by Christ. They 'are a chosen people, a royal priesthood, a holy nation, a people belonging to God', who called them 'out of darkness into his wonderful light' (1 Pet. 2:9). We are called to leave behind the standards of the world and to submit ourselves to valuation by Christ. Paul offers himself as a living example of someone who has tried to do this, setting to one side the values of the world and living according to the standards of Christ (Phil. 3:17–21).

At an awkward moment in his career, Paul was called upon to give an account of himself before the Roman authorities. He did so by establishing his credentials in a manner calculated to impress his hearers. 'I am a Jew, from Tarsus in Cilicia, a citizen of no ordinary city' (Acts 21:39). Here Paul exploits the natural human tendency to value people on account of their origins. Members of prominent families often find that they can use the status of their pedigrees to gain access to important social circles. In much the same way, academics associated with Oxford or Cambridge in the United Kingdom or with Ivy League universities in the United States discover that their prestige is generally considerably enhanced by this attachment. Paul used the same strategy shortly afterwards when he impressed the Roman tribune with an appeal to his origins. Once the tribune discovered that Paul was born with the right to Roman citizenship (Acts 22:25–29), he treated Paul with considerable deference.

In his letter to the Philippians, Paul stresses that Christians have status, not on account of the city in which they were born, but on account of the city to which they have been called. Christians are citizens of the new Jerusalem: 'our citizenship is in heaven. And we eagerly await a Saviour from there, the Lord Jesus Christ' (Phil. 3:20).

Paul develops this idea by drawing on an image familiar to the Philippians. Philippi was not an independent city but a Roman colony under the rule and military authority of Rome. Although located in northeastern Macedonia, the city obeyed the laws and customs of Rome rather than those of Macedonia. Paul's image is enormously helpful in connection with Christian self-esteem. The church is like a Roman colony. It is located in the world, but does not conform to its standards. Instead, it looks to its homeland for its values. It learns to set the same estimation upon individuals and achievements as those which hold sway in the new Jerusalem. The world often does not share those standards, but judges and assesses people on the basis of their achievements, possessions, social status and circumstances of birth. However, like a colony in the midst of an alien land, the church must learn to treat such outlooks with scepticism and not be overwhelmed by them.

Christians can rest assured and be confident in their future status as renewed, forgiven and transformed individuals on account of the faithfulness of God. Present self-esteem rests upon God's past acts of redemption and his promise of future transformation. Christ, Paul stresses, 'will transform our lowly bodies so that they will be like his glorious body' (3:21). In other words, we shall finally be *with* Christ and *like* Christ. And in the light of that knowledge, we may value ourselves positively in the present.

Knowing this, we may anticipate the future status this will bring. We are not made perfect yet – but that future status is promised us with the resurrection from the dead. We are not being asked to achieve this unaided, but instead to trust in the power and faithfulness of God: 'for it is God who works in you to will and to act according to his good purpose' (2:13).

Being taken hold of by Christ

Paul does not consider the faithfulness of God to be something passive; it is through God's faithfulness that he grasps us and holds us firmly. Being firmly attached to Christ allows us to turn our attention to the tasks and concerns of the life of faith, without continually worrying about our status in the eyes of the world. 'I press on to take hold of that for which Christ Jesus took hold of me' (3:12). Paul here sees himself as being embraced or enfolded by Christ, just as he will elsewhere talk about the Christian being 'in Christ'.

Paul's use of the language of attachment helps to cast light on the issue of Christian self-esteem. Just as a child feels secure when 'attached to' a parent, so the children of God experience peace and security by being taken hold of by Christ. To be 'in Christ' is thus to be held firmly and compassionately in a relationship with Christ. What the world thinks of us becomes unimportant, when held in the loving care of Christ.

As we have seen, the coming of Christ itself is a dramatic and powerful challenge to the world's standards, especially to the manner in which it esteems people. For example, Aaron Beck argues that our self-esteem should rest upon external achievements. Carl Rogers rejects this, arguing that we should not become dependent upon external achievements or the judgment of others. But what is to be put in their place? Upon what is self-esteem to be based? Paul argues that the ultimate ground of our self-esteem is our being 'in Christ', with all that this entails.

Christians need not be held captive to the worldly views of esteem. The words of Isaiah, foretelling the coming of Christ, are worth careful thought:

> He was despised and rejected by men,
>   a man of sorrows, and familiar with suffering.
> Like one from whom men hide their faces
>   he was despised, and we esteemed him not.
>
> (Is. 53:3)

The world did not esteem Christ; on the contrary, it despised him because, by its standards, he was weak and shameful. Yet in the end it was Christ who judged the world, not the world that judged Christ. Christians must have confidence in Christ, and not feel intimidated or oppressed by the low esteem in which they are held by the world. Nor must they feel that they must give in to the world's pressure to esteem people in terms of their achievements or possessions. Our righteousness is grounded in Christ, not in anything that we or the world can do or think.

And in the light of this knowledge, Paul again affirms the Philippian Christians. They are to value themselves as Paul values them. 'Therefore, my brothers, you whom I love and long for, my joy and crown, that is how you should stand firm in the Lord, dear friends!' (4:1). Wrongly understood, this could lead to complacency. But for Paul, proper Christian self-esteem is a bulwark against despair and a sense of powerlessness. If Christians are to work well and effectively for God, they need to know that God values what they are doing and is able to do great and wonderful things through them. Proper Christian self-esteem is grounded in God's love and care for us. It does not presume upon God, for example, by naïvely trusting in our ability to cope without God or to redeem ourselves or others by our own powers. Rather, it means attaching ourselves to God in faith and trust, in the knowledge that he can make up for our deficiencies and use us in his service.

Perhaps the most famous statement of this view is found in Paul's reflections on his 'thorn in the flesh'. We are not entirely clear what this 'thorn' was; nevertheless, Paul's interpretation of it is clear. It was given to him by God, to keep him 'from becoming conceited' (2 Cor. 12:7). As a result, he learned that, despite his weakness, God was indeed able to value and use him. God's words to Paul summarize all that needs to be said here, 'My grace is sufficient for you, for my power is made perfect in weakness' (2 Cor. 12:9). Paul thus felt able to boast of his weakness, knowing that the power of Christ might rest upon him. 'I can do everything through him who gives me strength' (Phil. 4:13).

Secular self-esteem involves valuing oneself over and against God; Christian self-esteem involves valuing oneself in and through Christ. A high worldly self-esteem can lead to pride and arrogance and a deliberate refusal to depend upon God. It is like a tower of Babel, a monument to human self-satisfaction in defiance of God. Christian self-esteem involves recognizing that God's strength is made perfect through our weakness, being willing to have status in the sight of God rather than in the sight of the world or of ourselves.

Joy and peace: being content in Christ

In the final chapter of his letter, Paul turns his attention to joy, the emotional result or spiritual fruit of the theological truths expounded above. Christians are to rejoice, whatever their situation. 'Rejoice in the Lord always. I will say it again: Rejoice! Let your gentleness be evident to all. The Lord is near. Do not be anxious about anything' (4:4–6). Paul develops this point in his famous declaration about his personal circumstances, 'I have learned to be content whatever the circumstances' (4:11). But how is this to be done? How can we rejoice, when our situation often seems hopeless or useless? For Paul, the key to peace and rejoicing lies in trusting in God, and accepting God's estimation of ourselves and our situation – not basing our estimation of our status and situation on human judgments.

Paul can be content in all circumstances because his self-esteem is not ultimately based upon his situation, pedigree or achievements. His self-esteem is grounded in his attachment to Jesus Christ – which nothing can destroy. 'For to me, to live is Christ, and to die is gain' (1:21). The strength of this attachment is such that he need not be anxious about anything, but he can rest in the peace of God. Anxiety arises through over-investment in our achievements and personal circumstances; peace arises from attachment to God through Christ. Paul has thus 'learned the secret of being content in any and every situation, whether well fed or hungry, whether living in plenty or in want' (4:12).

Being content in all circumstances leads to peace. Paul sets aside false expectations in order to focus on Christ and to know his peace and joy. In urging his readers to ground their self-esteem in Christ, Paul assures them that they will have a peace inaccessible to those who look to the world for their security and standards. A self-esteem that is grounded outside of Christ will be a constant source of anxiety. People change their minds; fashions change; what was in today will be out tomorrow. Paul offers us the ultimate – indeed, for the Christian, the only – basis of genuine positive self-esteem: the knowledge that we have been united to Christ through faith and that nothing – not even death – can sever this link. A self-esteem based on worldly foundations will lack the serenity and constancy of that which is based in Christ, who is 'the same yesterday and today and for ever' (Heb. 13:8).

Conclusion

In drawing this chapter to a close, let us return to the four areas from which self-esteem is drawn, and see how they relate to the gospel proclamation of redemption through Christ. In each case, we shall contrast secular and Christian approaches to the question.

Pedigree. The gospel declares that we are bonded to Christ through faith. We are adopted into the family of God and have come to share the same family tree as other believers, which can be traced back to the great names of the Bible, such as Abraham, Isaac and Jacob.

Love of another. It is not merely that we are attached to Christ though faith. The grounds of that attachment – in other words, that which makes this attachment possible in the first place – is the death of Christ upon the cross, which the New Testament insists arises directly from the love of God for us. Love both makes that attachment possible and expresses itself in that attachment.

Performance of roles. In secular eyes, this refers to the ways in which the love of others can be earned. But the gospel does not present the love of God as something that can be earned. The doctrine of grace declares that God himself has done everything necessary to allow us to become attached to him through faith. The roles we are being asked to perform are those of obedience, faith and love – but these roles do not *earn* the love of God; they *express* the love of God.

Eternal significance. As Ernst Becker pointed out in his important work *The Denial of Death* (1973), much of western culture is dedicated to preserving the illusion that death does not happen, or to extending physical life for as long as possible, in part due to the negative impact of the thought of death upon human pride and self-esteeem. But the gospel has another solution. Christian self-esteem, as we saw, is grounded in our union with Christ, which nothing can destroy. If anything, death merely draws us closer to God by snapping the final bonds that link us to this fallen world of sin.

This chapter has focused on the self-esteem of the individual. However, the community of faith also has an important role to play in the nourishing and fostering of a proper Christian self-esteem. In the chapter that follows, we shall consider ways in which the church community can help its members to know the peace and joy that Paul commends.

8

Encouragement in Christ: the life of the church

In this concluding chapter, we shall explore some implications of the ideas developed in this book for the life of the Christian church. How do all these ideas work out in the life of the church? How can we help people to value themselves? Obviously, the main emphasis of what follows will relate to Christian counselling and interpersonal relationships. However, it is also important to learn to see the church as a healing community. We have already noted Augustine of Hippo's famous image of the church as a hospital, and we explored the parallels between sin and physical illness. It is now time to apply some of the insights explored in this work.

The need to affirm people

Throughout this work, we have stressed the importance of affirmation. People need to feel that they are valued. We see precisely this principle of affirmative interaction in the ministry of Jesus, the foundational role model for Christians.

Acceptance

In his actions and his words, Jesus affirms people through

accepting them. Many theologians have made the point that Jesus, in his personal ministry, embodies the idea later identified in theological terms by Paul – justification by faith. Jesus is prepared to accept those whom the world regards as unacceptable. He sits at table with those whom the world regarded as outcasts, such as tax collectors, the menial puppets of the Roman authorities. He mingles with those with whom respectable people would have no dealings, such as prostitutes. He was seen alone with women – a scandalous matter at the time – and talked to them as equals about the wonders of the kingdom of God (note the amazement of the disciples at this in John 4:27). He preached to Samaritans, to the horror of the Jews. He mingled with, spoke to, and even touched lepers, who had been cast out by society as unclean (Mark 1:40–42), risking becoming leprous himself. In short, Jesus was prepared to meet and accept even those whom society regarded as outcasts.

This acceptance is not an end in itself. It leads to the alteration of life. Perhaps the most striking example of this may be found in the story of Zacchaeus (Luke 19:1–10). He was a tax collector, viewed with utter contempt by his fellows. His low social status was compounded by the fact that he was small. With a few choice phrases, Luke persuades us that we are dealing with a man who was treated like dirt by society.

Yet Jesus invited himself to Zacchaeus' house to share a meal. The enormously affirmative character of Jesus' personal attitude towards the tax collector is evident from the joy with which Zacchaeus received him. Yet the story does not end there. Jesus' affirmation of Zacchaeus led to his repentance. 'Look, Lord! Here and now I give half of my possessions to the poor, and if I have cheated anybody out of anything, I will pay back four times the amount' (verse 8). It was only then that Jesus declared that the restoration and healing was complete. 'Today salvation has come to this house' (verse 9).

Following Jesus means accepting outcasts. There is no escape from the call to engage in the world outside the church. What is required is not merely positive social action, not only prophetic preaching, but also the establishment of personal affirming relationships with those whom the world devalues or rejects. This is a costly business. The world may reject people precisely because they are unlovable in the conventional sense. Those who have been used to rejection in the past often test out relationships by behaving in demanding or outrageous ways. For this reason it is important that *networks* of caring relationships, rather than intense one-to-one relationships, are developed so that Christians can support one another, practically and in prayer, through emotionally difficult times.

Knowing

It will be recalled from chapter 3 that one of the characteristics of a good therapist is accurate empathy – having an understanding at both the emotional and intellectual levels of the other person's situation. In counselling and psychotherapy this is achieved by listening carefully to the client. Good listening is far more difficult than it appears, requiring an enormous amount of concentration. It takes time and training to develop good listening skills. They are a necessary requirement for therapy to proceed because they allow the therapist to reach a psychological *understanding* of the problem – the *formulation*. The respect shown by taking the trouble to listen properly also establishes a collaborative bond between the client and the therapist. This process cannot be rushed.

When Jesus met people he did not have the luxury of several hours' private consultation in which to take a life history, investigate the current 'presenting problem', or to create a therapeutic bond. But, of course, he did not and does not need this. He knows us intimately already because he is our creator (Ps. 139; John 8:56), and he understands our situation because he too has been a human being (Matt. 1:23; Heb. 4:15).

Jesus' acceptance of people is not based on ignorance of them and their circumstances. This fact should speak powerfully to people with avoidant personalities who believe that if people knew what they were really like, they would reject them. Time and time again, we find people commenting on how Jesus seemed to see right to the heart of their very being. A particularly touching feature of the story of Zacchaeus discussed above is that Jesus called Zacchaeus by his name (see also John 10:3).

This theme of knowing is particularly characteristic of John's Gospel. Jesus 'knew all men' (John 2:24). Amazed at and transformed by what Jesus had told her about herself, the Samaritan woman at the well said to all her friends, 'Come, see a man who told me everything I ever did. Could this be the Christ?' (John 4:29). Jesus' first encounter with Nathanael (John 1:47–51) hinges on Nathanael's astonished, 'How do you know me?' (1:48), followed immediately by his confession that Jesus is the Son of God.

Jesus is one who knows people, and is able to discern the inner thoughts and concerns of those to whom he ministers. We need to be his followers in this respect also. Knowing people means spending time with them, listening carefully and, crucially, giving them permission to reveal their weaknesses to us. We can do this by being frank about our own weaknesses and by communicating that our acceptance of them is, like Christ's, unconditional. We may see a need for radical change in their lives, and we may see a need to persuade them of this, but through it all our love for them should remain constant. These principles apply most clearly in the realm of parenting, but are not confined to parent–child relationships by any means.

Affirming people in prayer

Praying *for* people is in itself highly affirmative, in that it indicates that we value them. Yet praying *with* people can be even more affirming, especially if thought is given to the way we pray. Our prayers for people indicate how we feel about them. Praying affirmative prayers with others can be enormously helpful. Perhaps the most obvious way of doing this is by giving thanks for them, listing their helpful or inspiring qualities and gifts. Prayer not only draws us closer to God; it draws us closer to each other.

Affirming people through preaching

Some pastors adopt a strongly exhortative style of preaching, which stresses the inadequacies in their congregations and aims to shame people into more effective Christian ministry and lifestyles.

However, a strongly critical approach can reinforce the negative self-esteem of some members. Paradoxically, from the standpoint of the preacher, it thus becomes self-defeating. Some of the congregation will become so demoralized that they will regard themselves as incapable of the required improvements.

Exhortation needs to be tempered with affirmation. Often the reason individuals are less effective disciples than they might be is that they lack confidence. Heavy styles of exhortative preaching often destroy what little confidence they have and make them even less likely to reach spiritual maturity. We have already noted the strongly positive impact of the affirmative ministry of Jesus on those he encountered. It must be stressed that affirmation in no way excludes exhortation; it merely sets that exhortation in its proper context.

The following biblical passages are examples of texts that are eminently suitable for affirmative preaching styles:

Psalm 103:13–18. Note the emphasis upon God's compassion for the weakness and frailty of his children and the affirmation of his steadfast love.

1 Corinthians 1:26–31. Paul emphasizes that God deliberately chooses to call those regarded as weak and foolish, in order that God's strength and wisdom may be made known through them.

2 Corinthians 4:7. The imagery of 'treasure in jars of clay' indicates that there is no contradiction in the entrusting of something enormously precious to something down-to-earth and common.

2 Corinthians 12:8–10. Note the affirmation of the ability of God to use those who are weak, and the superb declaration that the power of God is made perfect in weakness.

Philippians 2:12–13. The exhortation to believers to work out their salvation is coupled with the vital affirmation that God is at work within them, empowering and enabling them to achieve this goal.

1 Peter 2:9–10. The calling of believers is emphasized, along with the privileges it brings. Despite all their weaknesses and inadequacies, Christians are chosen, royal, and holy, called to declare the love of God to the world.

Many more such passages might be noted; the above are

intended to illustrate, rather than exhaust, the possibilities open to preachers. The following basic themes, which are highlighted by these passages, are of major importance in developing affirmative styles of preaching, and they must be given due consideration:

- God knows that we are weak and frail.
- God has entrusted the precious gift of his gospel to us; he has placed the treasure of the gospel in vessels of clay.
- God's strength is made perfect in human weakness.
- The grace of God is sufficient for us.
- We are not to trust in our own abilities, but in Christ's; self-reliance can thus be a serious barrier to relying on God.

Fostering an awareness of attachment to Christ

As we have argued throughout this work, the basis of Christian self-esteem is our union with Christ. Christian self-esteem is grounded in our relationship with Christ, established through faith on the basis of the cross of Christ. To rephrase this, it is grounded in our attachment to Christ, which is made possible through his saving death and resurrection. Luther spoke of 'a grasping faith' (*fides apprehensiva*), by which the believer takes hold of Christ and becomes attached to him.

Maintenance of a positive and authentically Christian self-esteem will depend upon effective presentation of our 'attachment to Christ' through faith, as well as on the fostering and nourishing of this union by every possible means. The preacher should draw attention to central New Testament images relating to salvation that incorporate the notion of attachment to Christ. We look at two of these images here; we shall explore others later.

The Body of Christ. The New Testament frequently refers to the community of believers – those who have been called out of the world as the church – as 'the body of Christ'. 'Now you are the body of Christ, and each one of you is a part of it' (1 Cor. 12:27). The image of the body suggests the idea of being connected in an organic unity. Christ is the head of that body (Col. 1:18). The imagery here is that of a group of people permanently and organically attached to Christ as their living head.

This has implications for our perception of status. Paul stresses that the lesser members are just as much a part of that body as those considered more important (1 Cor. 12:12–26). Each member must value other members, despite their different functions, and the apparently different status of those functions. All the parts of the body are organically connected, making up a greater whole. What gives the Christian body both its spiritual life and its unity of nature and purpose is its connection to Jesus Christ. We value each member as we see him or her as linked to Christ. This idea is developed further in Paul's powerful image of 'being in Christ'.

Being in Christ. 'Therefore, if anyone is in Christ, he is a new creation' (2 Cor. 5:17). To be a Christian is to be in Christ – that is, to be connected and attached to him, as a bride is attached to her husband and a husband to his bride. This forceful image stresses that Christian faith represents far more than believing in Christ; it is about entering into Christ, possessing him and being possessed by him. Faith is about the forging of a bond of unity that goes far beyond mere belief. In its most profound sense, as we saw earlier, it is about grasping Christ and becoming part of him. The New Testament's images of being 'born again' (e.g. John 3:3) stress the transformative aspects of this process of being united to Christ through faith.

These, then, are some of the ways in which the notion of attachment to Christ can be explained and justified theologically. But what of nurturing an awareness of this attachment with a view to enhancing it? Some suggestions for developing a closer attachment may be of some use.

Make more effective use of the sacraments. One of the ways of assimilating something is to eat it – to make it part of our bodies by the process of digestion. This imagery is used by Christ himself to emphasize the intimate nature of his relationship with his disciples: … 'unless you can eat the flesh of the Son of Man and drink his blood, you have no life in you. Whoever eats my flesh and drinks my blood has eternal life, and I will raise him up at the last day' (John 6:53–54). This powerful metaphor of attachment is very comforting to many Christians, who find eating the communion bread and drinking the communion wine a deeply evocative reminder of both the cost of their redemption and the closeness of their relationship with Christ.

Similarly, baptism emphasizes the closeness of the attachment between Christ and the believer. Baptism unites us with Christ in his death and resurrection (Rom. 6:1–11; Col. 2:12). We are being reminded that 'If we have been united with him like this in his death, we will certainly be united with him in his resurrection' (Rom. 6:5).

Evangelicals have traditionally not regarded the sacraments as having a significant role in pastoral ministry. This may represent the loss of an important insight. For example, the sacraments play a vital role in Reformation spirituality. Luther urged us to see the sacraments as 'promises with signs attached', the idea being that the physical aspects of the sacraments would bring home to us dramatically and effectively the spiritual message of the gospel. The communion service can be a deeply moving and powerful reminder of our need to feed on Christ, and thus deepen our attachment to him. The very act of extending an empty open hand to receive the communion bread is a forceful reminder that we come to Christ in our emptiness, to feed on his richness. The sacraments offer us physical images of attachment, enabling us to visualize its importance and the benefits it brings.

Make more effective use of analogies of attachment in the everyday world. Such analogies might be drawn, for example, from the realm of personal relationships or from nature.

An obvious example of attachment drawn from personal relationships is marriage. Luther uses this image to great effect in *The Liberty of a Christian* (1520), in which he argues that 'faith unites the soul with Christ as a bride is united with her bridegroom'. Faith is a 'wedding ring' (Luther), pointing to mutual commitment and union between Christ and the believer.

This powerful image fits in superbly with a group of major biblical images of sin. Sin is like divorce (Is. 50:1) – a formal separation between God and his people. Yet this separation is ended through repentance and faith. Sin is like widowhood (Is. 54:4) – again, an image of separation between God and his people, with the inevitable attendant mourning and grief. Sin is about being 'shut out from the presence of the Lord and from the majesty of his power' (2 Thess. 1:9), just as salvation is about being restored to that presence. The preacher can make effective use of such imagery in drawing attention to the need to be united to Christ in the life of faith.

An example of an image from the natural world is Christ's use of the notion of attachment in his image of the vine (John 15:1–11). 'I am the true vine,' Christ told his disciples (verse 1). He develops the image of himself as the vine and of his disciples – those who have been redeemed – as branches. Their well-being is totally dependent upon their attachment to him: 'apart from me, you can do nothing' (verse 5). If they become detached from him, they can no longer draw upon the life-giving sap he provides. Just as branches that are detached from the vine wither and die, so those who become separated from Christ will die spiritually (John 15:6).

The creative preacher can exploit such rich images further, as well as developing others that make the same point in a powerful visual manner. A picture is worth a thousand words: the use of such visual images will enable a congregation to grasp the importance of attachment to Christ for the Christian life far more effectively than the most intricate of theological arguments.

Affirming people through teaching

Responsible teaching – which may come through preaching or other sources, such as church study groups or Bible studies – can play a vital part in affirming people, especially those with negative self-esteem. We shall consider one area in which many people need help to think through issues of faith with a direct relevance to self-esteem: the valuation of achievement.

Many people tend to attribute all their successes to God and their failures to themselves. In one sense, this is understandable, in that it mirrors some important scriptural insights (most notably, relating to humility). However, it can also be unhelpful and runs the risk of seriously distorting aspects of the gospel message. Let us see how this happens.

God values us! That is one of the central themes of the doctrine of grace. Too often we hear only the negative side of the gospel –

that we, as unworthy sinners, can do nothing worthwhile in the sight of God. We cannot achieve our own salvation. The words of Augustus Toplady's famous hymn 'Rock of Ages', probably written about 1775, express this feeling well:

> Nothing in my hand I bring,
> Simply to thy cross I cling;
> Naked, come to thee for dress;
> Helpless, look to thee for grace;
> Foul, I to the fountain fly;
> Wash me, Saviour, or I die.

Yet the doctrine of grace is not intended to humiliate us. It is meant to bring us to our senses. It is meant to deflate any ideas we might have of our ability to earn our salvation. It is only by bringing home to us the hopelessness of our situation that God can persuade us to turn to him.

The doctrine of grace, rightly understood, is about *valuing* achievements, but *not relying upon them*. Achievements become a threat to the life of faith when they are seen in a false light – as the basis of our salvation, rather than as its natural consequence. Grace denies that we *earn or achieve* our salvation, and affirms the need for effort and commitment on our part as a response to what God has done for us. Achievements – the 'works' of James 2:14–26 – are the fruit of faith. And they are to be valued, just as the fruit of a tree or vine is to be valued. The image of the vine (John 15:1–11) makes it clear that the fruit of the vine is to be valued and appreciated, and encouraged to grow. Yet that fruit is a result of being attached to Christ, not the precondition or basis of that attachment.

Our achievements are rightly seen as being due to God. Nevertheless, they are something that God chooses to achieve *through us*. Our achievements are themselves the gift of God. In recognizing that they are *due* to God, we must also recognize that they have been achieved *through* us. There is a synergy – a working together of God and ourselves. The image of a yoke is profoundly important in this context (see Matt. 11:28–30). In biblical times, a strong and a weak animal were often yoked together. The stronger animal could enable the weaker to achieve tasks which, on its own, the latter could never have accomplished. Believers are yoked together with God, who enables us to achieve things that otherwise would be impossible. Both God and the believer are at work together (Phil. 2:12–13); the fact that God is by far the dominant partner in this relationship should not prevent us from recognizing that God allows us to make a real contribution to what is achieved through us. To believe in God's grace is to deny that we can earn salvation and to learn to trust God in the efforts we make for him. The notion of a partnership with God in the service of the gospel is itself profoundly affirming.

We need to *value* our own achievements – not to *boast* in them, but to value them as something God regarded as worth achieving in and through us. The parable of the talents makes this point powerfully (Matt. 25:14–30). God allows us to share in his purposes and exalts us, partly by what he does in and through us. But we must also learn to value the achievements of others, both for what they are in themselves and for the benefits that they bring to the life of the church as a whole. God's gifts are blessings given for the building up of the Christian community, and it is right that we should honour and value the Giver, the gifts and those to whom they are given.

This might seem to imply that there is no room for under-achievement or failure in God's church. Yet this is to overlook a major scriptural theme already discussed in chapter 4 – that God works in and through failure too. This point is reinforced in 2 Corinthians 12:7–10, in which Paul speaks of a 'thorn in the flesh', which was given to him in order to humble him and teach him that God's strength is made perfect in weakness. Failure can be a way in which God humbles us and makes us *teachable*. Indeed, one of the genuine tensions between Christianity and the prevailing secular culture relates to the manner in which they accommodate failure.

The teacher must also be alert to unhelpful patterns of attribution within his or her congregation. Negative self-esteem may reflect inaccurate patterns of attribution. For example, the attribution, 'I failed in that task because I am useless', should be challenged. A more accurate attribution might be, 'I failed in that task because it was too difficult.' Individuals should be helped to explore their own cognitive styles with a view to allowing them to see the world through less distorting spectacles.

In *The Psychology of Religious Knowing* (1994: 117), Fraser Watts and Mark Williams emphasize the importance of such considerations: 'People seldom check the validity of their attributions, with the result that a vicious spiral is set up in which greater emotional disturbance and isolation produce more maladaptive attributions and further mood disturbance.' The pastor should thus be alert to such possibilities in order to help people to identify their misattributions, to check them out and to change them to ones more realistic or helpful.

Thus far, we have considered the importance of affirmation in the life of the church. Yet a possible criticism may be noted at this point. It might be objected that affirmation is potentially uncritical, in that it fails to address a person's faults, weaknesses and sin. However, as discussed earlier in this chapter, affirmation of individuals does not rule out any attempt to redirect them. Affirmation does not necessarily entail leaving people unchanged. The idea of non-directive affirmation finds no support in the ministry of Jesus. Whoever heard of a non-directive shepherd telling his sheep to do whatever seemed good to them?

Perhaps the classic example of Jesus' affirmative and directive ministry can be seen in his handling of the rich ruler (Mark 10:17–27). Mark tells us that Jesus *loved* this man. Yet (or perhaps because of this) he was strongly directive and behavioural in his approach. 'Go, sell everything you have and give to the poor, and you will have treasure in heaven. Then come, follow me' (verse 21). Again, in the case of the woman taken in adultery, Jesus is directive, 'Go now and leave your life of sin' (John 8:11). Even though Jesus refuses to condemn her for her sin, he nevertheless redirects her. Affirmation of people does not mean *leaving* them where they are; it means *meeting* them where they are – wherever that may be, and however distasteful that may sometimes be – and moving them on in love.

Also note that Jesus provided an answer to problems that may have originated in the past by firmly fixing people's attention on the here and now. For example, in the case of the man born blind (John 9:1–12), Jesus firmly directs attention away from the past (the man's sin or that of his parents) in order to focus attention on the present (his own forgiving and healing presence). It is often helpful and interesting to look for the origins of people's current problems in their early childhood experiences. However, this can become a distraction, keeping the person from dealing with current life problems. People need to feel that they are valued here and now, if they are to cope with problems inherited from the past. Jesus' meeting with the blind man provides a model of this affirmative mode of encounter.

This need for affirmation comes out clearly from the New Testament's stipulations on criticism within the Christian community.

Criticism and self-esteem

Criticism is easy to give and hard to take. Many people feel that life would be a lot easier if there were a worldwide moratorium on criticism. All too often, criticism seems to be a way in which other people destroy our sense of self-worth or break down self-confidence. Criticism can easily become a means of scoring points off people, making those who give it feel good about themselves and those who unwillingly receive it feel utterly despicable.

Yet criticism is an indispensable aspect of Christian living. Rightly used, it can be a vital stimulus to self-examination and personal growth. It is an essential element of Christian pastoral ministry, in which those who minister are able to help those for whom they care discover their strengths and weaknesses and do something about them. We all need an outside perspective if we are to discover how people really feel about us, instead of relying upon our own biased and distorted perceptions of what we are like. As many psychologists have pointed out, we have a tendency, through defence mechanisms, to think that we are perfect, popular and appreciated. And this often blinds us to the fact that we are actually not like that at all, and prevents us from discovering ways of becoming better people. Criticism can be a helpful way of discovering how things really are in order that we can begin to do something about it.

Love often expresses itself in criticism, just as a lack of care often gives rise to a lack of interest. But how can helpful and constructive criticism take place? How can we uphold people's self-esteem while helping them to recognize their weaknesses and faults? And how can we avoid the trap of criticizing others merely to make ourselves feel good? In what follows, we propose to lay down some theological principles for criticism grounded in the nature of God. It is inevitable that this discussion will pick up on points made elsewhere in this book; our concern here is to bring them together. Four points emerge as of decisive importance, both theologically and practically.

1. *Criticism is grounded in knowledge of the other person.* As we have seen, one of the reasons we feel able to trust God's judgment and valuation of us is that he knows us through and through. He has no delusions about us; nor can we keep any secrets from him. God 'knows the secrets of the heart' (Ps. 44:21). We are being criticized and judged by one who knows us totally. It is a realistic and reliable judgment on the part of one from whom we can have no secrets. That is the sort of person we feel good about taking criticism from. It is fair and informed.

But there is more to it than this. God judges us as one who knows what it is like to go through the cycle of human life with all its sorrows and pain. In Christ, God entered our world as one of us. He knows what it is like at first hand. That helps build up our confidence in the reliability of his judgment. It is much easier to take criticism from someone who knows what it is like to be human (Heb. 4:14–16).

Criticism within the Christian body must thus imply intimate knowledge of the other person. We know remarkably few people really well. A failure to know and understand individuals may make our criticisms of them unreliable and unhelpful. Criticism is a privilege; it is something that we can only do to those whom we know.

2. *Criticism implies commitment to the other person.* God has earned the right to criticize us. His credentials rest upon his being both our creator and our redeemer, one who has authority over us and who cares for us. Criticism is a privilege, which demands that the judge be committed to the judged. All we have said so far emphasizes that God is qualified to criticize us. He knows us

intimately; he cares for us; he has a vision for our future; and he is prepared to stand by us as we receive his power to reshape ourselves in line with that vision.

For, having criticized us, God does not abandon us. He does not present us with a list of failures and then leave us as we try desperately to improve ourselves. No. He remains with us, offering us his power, presence and promise as we try to bring our lives into line with the vision God sets before us in Christ. That means a lot of work on our part – but it is work that has been initiated, encouraged and supported by God. Paul expresses this relationship well: 'work out your salvation with fear and trembling, for it is God who works in you to will and to act according to his good purpose' (Phil. 2:12–13).

Criticism must thus be seen as a sign and a consequence of mutual care and commitment within the Christian body. It is too easy to judge someone harshly. Christ reminds us that the way we treat others will be reflected in the manner in which God treats us. Just as God may have some hesitation in forgiving individuals who are not themselves forgiving to others (Matt. 6:14–15), so he will judge us harshly if we are brutal with other believers. 'For in the same way you judge others, you will be judged, and with the measure you use, it will be measured to you' (Matt. 7:2).

3. *Criticism must be set within the context of affirmation.* We have already seen how the cross of Christ both affirms us and criticizes us. On the one hand, it tells us how much God loves us. 'God so loved the world that he gave his one and only Son' (John 3:16). The cross is the supreme demonstration of the love of God for us. It emphasizes to us how much we matter to him. It shows that we are dealing with a God who demonstrates his love in actions, rather than merely in words.

On the other hand, it criticizes us. It tells us that we are sinners. Although God loves us as we are, we are not what he would like us to be. We are challenged to become more like Christ. The cross brings home to us the fact that all are under the power of sin and that all are unrighteous in the sight of God (Rom. 3:9–10). None of us measures up to what God wants us to be. In the cross of Christ, we see the judgment of the world and ourselves.

The cross, then, makes known God's loving criticism of his

creation. It is a criticism tinged with sorrow and grounded in his care and compassion for us. God affirms us, telling us how much we matter to him, as he tells us that we are at best but pale shadows of what he would like us to be. But it is easier to take that criticism in the knowledge of his love and care for us. God graciously respects and preserves our self-esteem while motivating us to grow in grace in line with his will.

We should thus affirm and criticize one another at one and the same time. Criticism springs out of love for the other, not a desire to humiliate or score cheap points against someone. To judge someone is to aim to provide a vital, reliable and caring outside perspective that will enable the person to see himself or herself as others do. Yet this is done within the context of affirmation. Simply to criticize someone is to run the risk of reinforcing a sense of low esteem. It is potentially to encourage someone to believe that he or she is valueless. Affirmation gives the person hope and dignity. It not only makes such people more receptive to genuine criticism where this is appropriate; it heartens them and gives them hope that they can do something about their situation.

Even if offered with the best of intentions, criticism can easily destroy someone's frail sense of worth and dignity, often maintained with the greatest of difficulty under adverse circumstances. Thoughtless criticism can, quite simply, be destructive and negative. And just as God affirms us as he judges us, so we must take care to encourage, affirm and value those to whom we minister and those for whom we care.

4. *Criticism is not an end in itself.* God does not criticize us in order to humiliate us and leave us lying, battered and demoralized, in the dust. He breaks us down in order to build us up. God's condemnation is his penultimate word, not his final word. It is God's vision of what we could be that fires his criticism of what we now are.

Many Christian theologians stress that the first step in coming to faith in Christ is a knowledge of one's sin. It is only by becoming aware of the reality and seriousness of sin that we can come to discover the love and grace of God. God's judgment of us brings home the reality of sin as a necessary precondition for making us receptive to grace. It is only when we discover that we are condemned that we turn to seek forgiveness. It is only when we discover our emptiness that we turn to seek fulfilment from God. God's judgment exposes our inadequacy; God's grace makes us adequate.

Criticism must thus be seen as a means to an end, not an end in itself. Criticism can be little more than one person trying to beat another into the ground, asserting his or her superiority over the unfortunate victim. We noted in chapter 3 that people who themselves have fragile self-esteem seem to be over-ready to denigrate others. In the academic world, one of the cheapest forms of criticism is reviewing books. As Lewis W. Spitz, professor of history at Stanford University, once said: 'There are those who write. Those who can't write cut them down in reviews, which is one way of asserting themselves against their intellectual superiors.'

But criticism is not meant to be about boosting the egos of critics. Its proper function is to help people to grow and mature, discovering the gifts that God has given them, and enabling them to make the most of them in his service. The parable of the talents points to the fact that every believer has been gifted by God. It is vitally important that those gifts be identified and used to the full. Yet it is often difficult for individuals to identify their own gifts. An outside perspective is often essential. And it is here that a critic – in the best sense of the word – can be of real value. The outsider can help that person discover what his or her gifts are, as well as what they are *not*.

These, then, are four fundamental principles which underlie the way God judges us. They are invaluable and appropriate guidelines for Christian living. Paul urged his readers at Ephesus to 'Be imitators of God ... as dearly loved children' (Eph. 5:1). God has set us an example, which we would do well to imitate in our dealings with one another. Criticism must be seen as an act of *valuing* another, not of *humiliating* anyone.

Valuing one another

The Christian church should aim to provide an affirmative and accepting environment in which believers can grow in confidence. As we have already seen, acceptance and affirmation are not incompatible with criticism and correction.

There is, however, a natural human tendency to value high achievers, to the detriment of those who appear to have little to offer. Yet the kingdom of God turns our ideas of achievement and worldly order upside down – and in doing so, establishes a set of values which ought to be reflected and incorporated into the life of the church.

Perhaps the most familiar statement of these radical attitudes can be found in the Beatitudes, in which Christ identifies groups of people who are blessed (Luke 6:20–22). The categories listed invert the natural order: the poor, the hungry, those who weep and those hated by the world. In contrast, Jesus rebukes the rich, the full, those who laugh and those spoken well of by all. The church cannot be allowed to simply mirror the patterns of acceptance regarded as normal by the world; it must learn to accept and value those whom the world despises and disregards.

Some further illustrations of this principle will indicate its importance and scope.

1. The first will be last, and the last first (Matt. 19:30; 20:16). The order of precedence among human beings may well be totally inverted in the kingdom of God. Jesus criticized the natural human tendency to seek out places of honour, declaring that those who humbled themselves will be exalted (Luke 14:7–11).

2. Believers are called upon to be servants: 'whoever wants to be first must be your servant [lit. "slave"]' (Matt. 20:27; see also 23:11–12). Lordship implies servanthood, rather than an exemption from the obligation to serve.

3. In the parable of the great banquet (Luke 14:12–14), the invitation to the feast is thrown open to all, even to those whom the world despises: the poor, the maimed, the blind and the lame. The invitation to the feast is not based upon human status, or upon the desire for reward or social advancement.

4. James, in rebuking the natural tendency of churches to welcome well-dressed people while treating the shabbily dressed with scant regard, stresses that God has chosen the poor to be rich in faith. 'Has not God chosen those who are poor in the eyes of the world to be rich in faith and to inherit the kingdom he promised those who love him?' (Jas. 2:5). A similar point is made in relation

to the widow and her two copper coins (Luke 21:1–4).

This emphasis on the need to value every member of the church emerges naturally from the New Testament view that the church is the body of Christ. What gives the Christian body both its spiritual life and its unity of nature and purpose is its connection to Jesus Christ. This allows us – indeed, requires us – to value each member as we see him or her as linked to Jesus Christ. Paul stresses that the lesser members are just as much part of that body as those considered more important (1 Cor. 12:12–26). They are all organically connected, making up a greater whole.

It is not for one part of the body to assume that its function is superior to another; it must regard the well-being of the body as the supreme matter of importance and value the function of every member as it contributes to this.

Furthermore, it is the person, rather than merely his or her talents or achievement, who is to be valued. Affirmation must be set in the context of the whole person. 'I like your *achievement*' is a way of saying, 'I like *you*' – but we must not give the impression that we like that person only on account of those achievements. This affirmation must be a continual attitude on the part of the church, not simply an occasional happening. When Jesus was asked how often his disciples should forgive others, he replied, 'seventy-seven times' (Matt. 18:22). By this, he did not mean a mechanical repetition of forgiveness up to a specified limit. Rather, he meant that his disciples should embody a constantly forgiving attitude. In the same way, the church must be prepared to affirm its members continually, thus providing a protective and caring community within which believers, especially *weaker* members, may grow. The church members should be *available to, accepting of,* and *affirmative towards* each other.

But it may not be easy to affirm those who irritate and annoy us. The Christian must see Christ in other believers and value them accordingly. We are all in Christ (and can thus view each other with warmth and unconditional positive regard); yet we are all sinners (and can thus view each other with empathy and genuineness). 'If anyone says, "I love God," yet hates his brother, he is a liar. For anyone who does not love his brother, whom he has seen, cannot love God, whom he has not seen' (1 John 4:20).

Conclusion

The present work has shown how it is theologically possible and pastorally helpful to develop authentically Christian approaches to self-esteem. We have shown how theoretical and practical elements interact, allowing more effective ministry to those currently suffering from negative self-esteem. We have made suggestions for more thoughtful and helpful approaches to preaching and ministry. It is our hope that these approaches will help in the establishment of a nurturing environment, which can act as a secure base from which individuals can live out the effective Christian lives to which they are called in the world.

Appendix

Bible studies in self-esteem

The Bible is of fundamental importance to Christian life and thought, and it is therefore important to spend time reflecting on biblical passages which are of relevance to the themes of this book.

Each of the following biblical passages is important in relation to self-esteem issues. As you work through them, whether individually or in a group, you may find it helpful to ask how they illuminate these issues. For example, consider each of the passages below in relation to the following questions:

- In what way does this passage illuminate a specifically Christian approach to the issue of self-esteem?
- How would you apply its ideas in a counselling context?
- How could this passage be used in preaching?
- How does it help us to affirm people in a Christian manner?

Job 29. Note especially the impact of loss on Job's self-esteem. What do you think Job's self-esteem is actually based upon? How does this passage challenge us on this issue?

Psalm 31:1–3; Matthew 7:24–27. Both these passages use the image of a rock to illustrate the stability offered by trust in God. In what way does this biblical image relate to the 'secure base' identified by John Bowlby as being of such importance for self-esteem? And how does this cast light on properly Christian approaches to this issue?

Isaiah 53:1–12. This passage deals with the 'suffering servant', widely seen as an anticipation of the suffering and rejection of Christ (see 1 Pet. 2:21–24). Notice how *rejection* was an integral aspect of the mission of the suffering servant. What does this passage have to tell us about this? And how does this relate to self-esteem?

Matthew 25:14–27. This famous passage is usually known as 'the parable of the talents'. Why is the third servant criticized for concealing and not using his talent? What does this passage have to say about a Christian understanding of humility? How does this relate to self-esteem? What are the implications of this for counselling?

Luke 19:1–10; John 4:7–42. These two gospel passages describe Jesus' encounter with two very different people – Zacchaeus and 'the woman at the well'. What aspect of his way of relating to them seems to be of central importance here? What are the implications of this approach for Christian counselling? How does this relate to the approach to other Christians commended by Paul at Philippians 2:1–5?

John 6:51–58; 15:1–8. Both these passages contain images of attachment: eating bread, and being joined to a vine. Explain how each of these images helps us to appreciate the nature and importance of attachment. What are the benefits of attachment? And how does the image of the vine help us understand the consequences of becoming detached from Christ? Other biblical passages which are important here include Romans 8:35 (we cannot be separated from the love of Christ) and Philippians 3:20 (we are citizens of heaven, and will finally be with Christ for ever).

John 17:13–16. This important passage deals with the challenges that Christians can expect to face. The passage makes it clear that Christians cannot expect to be esteemed by the world, on account of their commitment to Christ. How should this expectation affect our thinking about our value and worth? What are the implications of being *in* the world, but not *of* the world?

Romans 5:1–5. Note the way in which this passage stresses the fact that our acceptance in the sight of God rests on what Christ has done, not on what we have achieved. Note also the emphasis on the fact that we have been accepted in Christ, and can thus have peace with God. You may find it helpful to examine other passages which stress that we have been accepted in Christ, such as 1 Corinthians 6:20 (we have been purchased at a price); Ephesians 1:5 (we have been adopted as God's lawful children) and Colossians 1:14 (we have been redeemed and forgiven).

Philippians 4:4–14. This passage brings out the importance of pedigree for human self-esteem, while at the same time stressing that the true self-worth of the Christian lies in Christ. How does Paul make this point?

Select bibliography

An asterisk (*) placed before a work indicates that it is a helpful introduction to the field.

Adams, Jay E. (1986). *The Biblical View of Self-Esteem, Self-Love and Self-Image*. Eugene, OR: Harvest House.

Anderson, Neil (1993). *Living Free in Christ*. Ventura, CA: Regal Books.

Baumeister, Roy F. (1986). *Identity: Cultural Change and the Struggle for Self*. Oxford: Oxford University Press.

Beck, A. T. (1989). *Cognitive Therapy and the Emotional Disorder*. Harmondsworth and New York: Penguin.

Becker, Ernst (1973). *The Denial of Death*. London: Free Press.

Bettelheim, Bruno (1960). *The Informed Heart*. New York: Free Press of Glencoe.

Bowlby, John (1969–82). *Attachment and Loss*. 2 vols. London: Hogarth.

*———— (1988). *A Secure Base*. London: Routledge.

Brown, G. W., & Harris, T. (1978). *The Social Origins of Depression*. London: Tavistock.

*Brown, J. A. C. (1969). *Freud and the Post-Freudians*. Harmondsworth and New York: Penguin.

158

Butler, Gillian, & Hope, Tony (1995). *Manage your Mind*. Oxford: Oxford University Press.

Carlson, David E. (1988). *Counseling and Self-Esteem*. Waco, TX: Word.

*Collins, Gary R. (1988). *Christian Counseling: A Comprehensive Guide*. Dallas, TX: Word.

Crook, John H. (1985). *The Evolution of Human Consciousness*. Oxford: Clarendon.

Dent, H., ed. (1987). *Clinical Psychology: Research and Developments*. Beckenham: Croon Helm.

Ellison, Craig W. (1983). *Your Better Self: Christianity, Psychology and Self-Esteem*. San Francisco: Harper and Row.

Fennell, Melanie (1999). *Overcoming Low Self-Esteem*. London, Constable Robinson.

Freud, Sigmund (1950). *Mourning and Melancholia* in *Collected Papers*, vol. 4. London: Hogarth.

Gilbert, P. (1992). *Depression*. Hove, Sussex: Lawrence Erlbaum.

Goffman, Erving (1968). *Asylums: Essays on the Social Situations of Mental Patients and Other Inmates*. Harmondsworth: Penguin.

Greenberger, Dennis, & Padesky, Christine (1995). *Mind over Mood*. New York: Guildford.

Hoekema, Anthony A. (1975). *The Christian Looks at Himself*. Grand Rapids, MI: Eerdmans.

*Hurding, Roger F. (1985). *Roots and Shoots: A Guide to Counselling and Psychotherapy*. London: Hodder and Stoughton.

Laing, R. (1960). *The Divided Self*. London: Tavistock.

Murray-Parkes, Colin, Stevenson-Hinde, Joan, & Marris, Peter (1991). *Attachment across the Life Cycle*. London, Routledge.

*Rogers, Carl R. (1961). *On Becoming a Person*. London: Constable.

Rutter, M. (1981). *Maternal Deprivation Reassessed*. Harmondsworth and New York: Penguin.

Schuller, Robert H. (1982). *Self-Esteem: The New Reformation*. Waco, TX: Word.

Smith, M. Blaine (1984). *One of a Kind: A Biblical View of Self-Acceptance*. Downers Grove, IL: InterVarsity Press.

Szass, T. (1972). *The Myth of Mental Illness*. London: Paladin.

Wagner, Maurice E. (1975). *The Sensation of Being Somebody: Building an Adequate Self-Concept*. Grand Rapids, MI: Zondervan.

Watts, Frazer, & Williams, Mark (1994). *The Psychology of Religious Knowing*. Cambridge: Cambridge University Press.

Wilson, Earl D. (1983). *The Discovered Self: The Search for Self-Acceptance*. Downers Grove, IL: InterVarsity Press.